SELF-HYPN... ...NTIFIC
SELF-SUGGESTION

by the same Author
THE THEORY AND PRACTICE OF HYPNOTISM (ARC)

self-hypnosis and scientific self-suggestion

William J. Ousby

ARC BOOKS, INC.
New York

Published 1969 by ARC Books, Inc.
219 Park Avenue South, New York, N.Y. 10003
Copyright © W. J. Ousby, 1966
Library of Congress Catalog Number 69-10759
Printed in U.S.A.

CONTENTS

FOREWORD by SIR PAUL DUKES, K.B.E.

Mr. Ousby's system will be of special interest to those who, while believing that hypnotism might well rid them of nervous troubles and wrong habits of living, would none the less hesitate to visit a hypnotist. If such people will persevere in carrying out the instructions given in these pages they will certainly be able to help themselves in ways of which they have never dreamed. During recent years, both in Britain and America, soldiers have been trained by using self-hypnotic techniques to render themselves immune from pain and even to undergo torture without betraying military secrets. The self-hypnotic trance is undoubtedly the secret which enables firewalkers and fakirs to perform their feats.

Mr. Ousby's presentation of the subject is eminently practical for use in everyday life. He is a scientific hypnotist skilled in the Eastern and Western techniques, and by profession a psychoanalyst. His aim is to show the essentially simple yet powerful working of the mind under suggestion, and the methods whereby its technique can be systematically applied to oneself while retaining full volitional control.

The key to success lies in the ability to implant suggestions in the unconscious mind. With this in view, the author has set forth a method of progressive physical relaxation through which control is gradually extended to mental and emotional mastery. The reader is shown how he is, in his present condition, actually hypnotising himself by his doubts and fears, and he learns how to reverse the process so that his subconscious mind diverts the elemental energy of his thoughts into constructive channels. Not the least merit of this Course is its profound sincerity. There is no doubt that the author is imbued with a deep desire to help all who are willing to make the initial effort to help themselves.

(signed) PAUL DUKES

INTRODUCTION

Broadly speaking, there are four groups of people who are aware of the tremendous power suggestion possesses to alter people's lives.

Firstly, the politicians, advertising and public relations specialists who influence public opinion.

Secondly, the individuals who have learned the subtle art of using this powerful force upon themselves through the self-suggestion or auto-hypnotic techniques.

Thirdly, those whose work is to treat with, and teach others how to use these techniques for gaining greater mental and emotional control and overcoming psychosomatic ailments.

Lastly, those who have come to realise they need assistance in freeing themselves from the influence of negative thought, worry or some psychosomatic ailment which defies all effort of will and logic to displace it.

It is my conviction that an individual who has had a nervous breakdown and dealt with it successfully is far better equipped to face life than someone who has never been through this experience. This is because in this critical battle for self-control, inner strengths and resources are revealed which otherwise would never have been discovered.

There is a story of ancient India which in allegorical form tells us something of the mysterious Unknown, or equally mysterious unconscious mind from which our mental and emotional life springs . . . and how in acquiring knowledge of the latent strengths and potentialities we all possess, we are also acquiring superior weapons for dealing with the problems we all have to face in life.

The story tells how Prince Arjuna, about to fight a critical battle, decides to go to the mountains to ask the God, Siva, for superior or secret weapons with which to win this battle. On the way, in a forest clearing, he sees a deer which he shoots for food, but at the moment he shoots, a stranger steps from the trees and also shoots the deer.

Arjuna, who by nature was proud and headstrong, angrily called out "You have no right to shoot the deer. I saw it first and it is mine." The stranger replied "You are foolish to think you can settle disputes by fighting, and if you are as bold as you are foolish, I must teach you a lesson." Arjuna's pride would not let him take back his arrogant words, and he could not avoid the challenge. So raising his bow he loosed an arrow at his opponent. To his amazement the stranger brushed his arrows aside. When Arjuna had fired all his arrows, he drew his sword but the stranger instantly disarmed him and held him in an iron grip like a helpless child. Disarmed and unable to move, Arjuna closed his eyes and humility took the place of arrogance and with passionate sincerity he prayed to the Gods to save him from his helpless plight.

As soon as Arjuna prayed for help he found himself free and unharmed and saw his adversary was Siva, who had manifested himself in human form as the embodiment of the human spirit.

In the story, Siva says, "I wanted to help you but you would not listen. You thought you could do everything unaided. Did you think the powers which created you had abandoned you? I wanted to give you superior weapons but you would not listen or ask me until I made you helpless."

Arjuna then realised that he was not a lonely figure battling against the Unknown but that forces stronger than himself could be called on to help him in his critical battle.

We, like Arjuna, by resolving our inner conflicts can free energy and unsuspected inner resources and so accelerate recuperative and healing powers; in short, turn the unconscious mind into a powerful ally which will aid us in living a healthier and happier life.

CHAPTER ONE

THE UNCONSCIOUS MIND

The following pages describe a simple "do it yourself" method of making alterations in oneself which cannot be achieved by will power alone. It goes beyond the simple reiterative principles of Coueism or any short-term methods of boosting will power.

These methods are successfully used to cure, prevent or alleviate a wide variety of complaints, but their application is not restricted to the remedial. They are being adopted as part of the personal techniques of many business and professional men and women, so that they may achieve greater efficiency with less wear and tear on the human machine.

A knowledge of natural laws is giving contemporary man ever increasing ability to harness and control electronic and atomic energy; in a similar way, an extension of his knowledge of laws governing mental and emotional energies gives him increased control over his own mental and emotional life. In the following pages it is shown how nervous energy can be diverted into constructive channels, instead of being fuzed off in damaging tensions or negative thoughts and emotions.

Most of us have witnessed the efforts of young children trying to write, faces screwed up, heads craned forward, shoulders hunched, tension in every limb and feature. During these ill co-ordinated efforts to make a few lines on paper with a pencil, about one hundred times the necessary energy is being employed. People suffering from nervous tension resemble these small children, but, unlike them, many will not correct their mistakes, and later, through not knowing how to relax inner tensions, ruin their health through well meant but wrongfully directed efforts.

Those who have acquired their own personal techniques of relaxing and using self-suggestion or auto-hypnosis, usually accomplish much more work than ordinary people, and in times of crisis or difficult circumstances can act with a cool, calm detachment. Sir Winston Churchill was an excellent example of mental control and personal technique. His competent handling of men and events arose out of his ability to maintain his own mental clarity, energy and zest for work, which in turn arose out of his ability to relax at will.

Sir Winston once asked if a certain man had the ability to relax and, on hearing that he had not, remarked "He will not last." This comment could be made of many business men. Nervous strain is inseparable from positions of responsibility today, and stress complaints are now occupational risks of those in executive positions.

Those people who had tremendous capacity for work and leadership—Caesar, Napoleon, Leonardo da Vinci, Gandhi, Schweitzer, Roosevelt, Nelson, Churchill, and numerous others, did not rely on "driving" themselves, but had developed more informed methods of achieving peak performances of any tasks they undertook. The list of their qualities is almost identical—they had unfailing confidence in themselves, unusual powers of mental concentration, retentive memories, the ability to influence others, unusual capacities for work, and the ability to sleep for short periods whenever they chose to do so.

It might be thought that these men were fortunate and that they had been endowed with outstanding qualities at birth, but in most cases this was not so—these qualities were discovered during periods of adversity.

They discovered:

(a) That the average man uses only a fraction of his real potential
(b) That they could make greater use of their own latent abilities
(c) That this could be achieved without plundering their reserves of energy.

Sometimes the handbook of a motor car contains a simple explanation of how the engine works. The simplest explanation of how "the human machine" operates is to assume that man has two minds, a conscious mind and an unconscious mind. These two minds are separated by some form of barrier or curtain. The conscious mind does the thinking and "willing" and behind the curtain which separates these two minds the unconscious mind, working quietly in the background, regulates the major part of the activities necessary for living. It transforms food and oxygen into tissues and energy. It regulates the routine functions, co-ordinating the activities of all the organs of the body, the heart, stomach, liver, lungs, etc. It superintends the maintenance and repairs which the body requires—broken bones will knit, torn flesh will heal, antitoxins will be manufactured to combat fevers and in addition to this, the unconscious mind also controls almost all the functions of the physical and emotional life—it has absolute power over the routine functions. Nature, it has been said, would not trust man to digest his food by his own efforts, because through his carelessness or forgetfulness he would soon starve to death. The unconscious mind, with robot-like efficiency, controls all the organic functions of the body and consciously man is unaware of all this complex inner activity. This arrangement leaves the conscious mind free to attend to activities in the outside world ... and the arrangement works very satisfactorily if nothing happens to upset the automatic activity of the unconscious mind.

Nervous tension is the most common cause of interference with what should be the smoothly co-ordinated operations of the unconscious mind.

The first intimation a man has that something is wrong may be a mild attack of indigestion, or he feels nervy and cannot relax, or maybe is not sleeping well. He may become aware that the robot unconscious mind is keeping tensions switched on and that he cannot get instructions through to it to switch off. This is the condition loosely described as nervous tension, and is the basic cause of most stress complaints.

Animals possess a much simpler nervous system and lead a less complicated life than we humans. Because of this we can see, by observing them in the wild state, what happens under stress. In Kenya I once saw a herd of zebra grazing quietly. Suddenly a lioness, which had crept near them under the cover of some undergrowth, made a charge, and as soon as she appeared in the open the whole herd galloped off. The lioness, failing to get within striking distance, soon gave up the chase. The zebra gradually slackened their pace and, as the lioness stopped, although they had only moved a short distance, they also stopped, and to my surprise began grazing again as though nothing had happened. It will illustrate how the physical and nervous system operates if we examine what happened to the zebra during this alarm.

As soon as an alarm is given, chemical and physical changes in the body take place at lightning speed. Sugar from the liver, together with secretions from the adrenal glands, is released into the blood stream; blood pressure rises, and the animal is poised, senses alerted, muscles tensed, ready for instant action either to take refuge in flight or to stand and fight ... all other body processes (such as digestion) which are not essential to deal with the emergency, are suspended. When the danger has passed, all tensions subside, digestive processes are resumed and all activities go back to normal.

Man has a much more complicated nervous system than the zebra, and because of this, and the demands of life today, his tensions do not switch off as easily as those of an animal. As a result, few people are immune from nervous tension, and the prevalence of these tensions can be gathered from the frequent statements by medical authorities that the major part of all illness is caused by unsolved and emotional problems ... that is, by nervous tension.

With many people today, the unconscious mind is in a semi-permanent state of alert, creating a wide variety of psychosomatic and nervous complaints, but it can be influenced to switch off unnecessary tensions and so allow the body's natural recuperative powers to restore the rhythm of physical, mental and emotional functioning and also, at the same time, to allow constructive self-suggestions to be implanted in the unconscious mind to deal with specific and individual problems. The potential scope and value of the hypnotic, auto-hypnotic and self-suggestion techniques in helping others and oneself, is only fully realised by those who have some experience of these techniques.

The famous scientist J. B. S. Haldane gives some indication of the promise these techniques have for mankind in the following comment: "Anyone who has seen even a single example of the power of hypnotism and suggestion must realise that the face of the world and the possibilities of existence will be totally altered when we can control their effects and standardise their applications as has been possible, for example, with drugs which were once regarded as equally magical."

The hypnotic and modern suggestion techniques are in the same position today as penicillin and other antibiotics were a generation ago. At that time many people desperately needed the help that these precious drugs could have given them, but not enough was known of their large scale manufacture to make them freely available. The self-hypnotic and self-suggestion techniques taught in the following pages have been a turning point in the lives of many people, not only in curing ailments but in overcoming the problems of everyday life.

CHAPTER TWO

"GETTING THROUGH" TO THE UNCONSCIOUS MIND

This section contains further comments about the unconscious mind and begins instructions on the first steps in making contact with it.

The average individual has many demands made on him. During the whole of his waking hours his eyes and ears are kept busy with a succession of sights and sounds, and, at the same time, a ceaseless stream of thoughts flows through his mind, as often as not accompanied by emotional activity.

Much of this activity is carried out by the unconscious mind, but frequently much more energy and effort than should be necessary is taken up in performing these activities. By giving a little attention to the way in which the unconscious mind can be influenced, vast improvements can be made in the way it performs any task.

Although not aware of it, everyone, by means of the unconscious mind, already performs extraordinarily complex activities. For example, a man walking down a busy street is thinking of some problem. There will be all the sights and sounds which go to make up the noise and distraction of a street. The man, busy with his own thoughts, will pay no attention to the noise or the shop windows or people passing, but should a friend come walking towards him, or should someone suddenly call his name, his thoughts will be instantly switched to his friend or to the person who has called out his name. Although he was not consciously aware of all the sights and sounds going on around him, his unconscious mind had been busy noting them all ... but like a good servant had not reported to him matters which were of no importance, in this way leaving his conscious mind free to attend to more important matters, while his unconscious mind attends to routine matters. In short, the unconscious mind of any reader, though he may never have thought about psychology, is already highly trained, and if he wishes, he can delegate to it many tasks which it can carry out much more efficiently than can be done by use of the conscious mind.

The success of all suggestion depends on gaining co-operation of the unconscious mind ... and if it is approached with sincerity and patience, it will allow man to tap energies he never dreamed he possessed, carry out feats which seemed impossible and cure complaints which had been regarded as hopeless, but this is dependent on his working *with*, and not *against* the laws which govern our being.

Whatever task faces one in life, whether it is to cure an illness, alter a habit, make a success of a job, or master the techniques of self-suggestion, there is no more important question than "How can I get the co-operation of my unconscious mind?"

Often when trying to influence his unconscious mind, a man may encounter obstacles. Sometimes when he exerts his will to influence his unconscious, he may discover there is in the structure of the mind, something which prevents his instruction "getting through." He may say to himself "I am not going to smoke another cigarette" but later finds he is still smoking; for some reason his instructions have failed to get through to his unconscious mind.

The man trying only with his will power and courage

to overcome his problem may think it is a defeat to admit he cannot force his unconscious mind to do what he WILLS—but he can, like Arjuna, acquire the superior weapons which will enable him to succeed.

We cannot force our unconscious to work for us, but we can get its aid by using more informed methods. These methods enable us to enlist the help of the positive elements in the unconscious mind which are themselves striving to restore harmonious functioning.

The task of getting suggestions through to the positive elements in the unconscious mind is simplified, if we think of our mental make-up as a business house with departments on different floors. On the first floor are the joint managers, the Intellect and the Will; these represent the conscious mind. On the lower floors are the workers who will carry out any orders they are given, and whose work it is to maintain the routine functioning of the emotional and physical life. These workers, broadly speaking, represent the unconscious mind. They are protected by a guard whose function is to prevent orders getting through to these workers, for they will do what they are told irrespective of what it is or who tells them. The guard is there to stop them, otherwise people after watching a TV programme would rush out and buy detergents, foods or anything else the scientifically designed suggestions of the TV advertising had instructed them to purchase.

Continuing this simplified picture of getting suggestions through to the workers in the unconscious mind, we first adopt the strategy of lulling the guard into a quiescent state and quietly passing messages to the helpful workers, who are themselves striving to correct whatever deviation there may be from a healthy happy life. The first step in lulling the guard is achieved by carrying out physical relaxation.

Though relaxing sounds simple, it is something which has to be learned and there is no one who cannot learn to relax, however tense he may be, if he is patient and persistent. Once the ability is acquired it is as though shutters have been drawn on the outside world and attention is turned inwards. Recuperative processes begin and energy replenishes tired muscles, energy levels rise, and the guard is lulled into a quiescent state, creating favourable conditions for administering self-suggestions.

The following instructions deal with General Relaxation which is a helpful condition for the creation of self-hypnosis or the state of maximum suggestibility. The object in view is to attain a physical state in which tension is absent. This state is brought about not by learning new things to do, but by stopping various activities which are already going on.

Some people will find that if they spend a minute or two in deep breathing before the relaxation session it helps them to unwind and to "let go" more rapidly. This does not apply to everyone, and by experiment you will see if it is helpful or otherwise to you personally.

The following exercises deal with the cultivation of relaxation, or "letting go" by cultivating muscular limpness. When the body is relaxed, mental and emotional activities are influenced by this physical relaxation and are also quietened down. These are the first steps in "letting go."

When a limb is relaxed it is limp. It will lie motionless and inert. If it were lifted, bent or moved by someone else, no resistance or rigidity would be detected. It will move easily as though it were a piece of limp rope.

This relaxation is employed naturally by many animals, of which the cat is a good example. The flaccid way in which it can let its muscles relax completely, is very instructive and helpful by way of illustration in carrying out the following exercises.

In speaking of relaxation, the term "letting go" has been used. The question might be asked: "Letting go of what?" The answer would be to let go the tensions which cause restlessness and lack of ease. The difficulty with many people is that they have become habitually tensed up, and this overactive state of their nerves has become their normal condition. They have forgotten how to "let go."

To achieve relaxation it is necessary to let the tensions die down—but, as we have said, the tense individual may not be fully aware of all the tensions in himself. Some of the signs are to be seen in frowns, blinking, restless movements, and a lack of repose. The first exercise is directed towards educating the individual to recognise tension in himself as the first step to removing it. When he can recognise its presence he can also recognise its absence. Relaxation is nothing more than the absence of tension.

If, during the first attempts, when carrying out the exercises, your attention is distracted by some imaginary stiffness, or awkwardness in posture, or involuntary swallowing, and the like, do not attempt to force these distractions out of your mind. They cannot be banished by a direct effort of the will. As far as possible, turn the whole of your attention to the detail of the particular exercise upon which you are engaged. You may fail a number of times, but if you persevere repeatedly, the distractions will gradually cease as the nervous activity, of which the irritations are merely symptoms, quietens down.

The messages which may be flashed into consciousness such as: "My neck is stiff," "My mouth is dry," and so on, are due to the overactive sensory nerves. The fidgeting, twitching and other movements are due to motor nerve impulses, which are consciously or unconsciously attempting to relieve the real or imagined irritation. Tension in some degree is always present, even when we think we are relaxed. Our purpose is to reduce this tension to a minimum so that the symptoms of this overactivity cease.

CHAPTER THREE

GENERAL RELAXATION

This section gives you basic instructions on physically relaxing, and using self-suggestions to increase your powers of positive self-suggestibility and the creating of a trance state in subsequent sessions. At this stage some beginners may feel doubtful about their powers of self-suggestibility; these doubts are not unnatural considering they have failed to use positive self-suggestion, but these doubts vanish as the Course proceeds. It is not that people lack the power to suggest to themselves . . . as is all too evident in the results of damaging self-suggestion. What they lack is the knowledge of how to *positively* employ this power of self-suggestion.

This General Relaxation Exercise may take some time and have to be repeated for a number of sessions, but later the trance state, or a vastly increased state of suggestibility can be created fairly quickly without the routine of relaxing. Every time you carry out these preliminary exercises you will benefit if you will incorporate the prescribed suggestions which are to be used at the termination of each session.

To begin your General Relaxation Sessions isolate yourself where you will not be disturbed. If there is a possibility of this, lock your door.

It is best to choose a time when there is as little noise as possible. If there are, or are likely to be, outside noises, use cotton wool or ear plugs to deaden these sounds. It is wise to choose a time when you are not too tired or worried, and there are no tasks requiring your attention immediately after your exercise session. In short, arrange matters, as far as possible, so that you have a free mind. To this end it will be found helpful if you can arrange to be quiet for an hour or so preceding the first sessions. After you have carried out the exercises several times, it will be found that these preliminary preparations are no longer required.

Make yourself comfortable on a couch or a bed with or without a pillow, as suits you best. Some people find that they can relax better on the floor with a carpet or a rug to lie on, but the reader after experimenting, will be the best judge of what suits his own needs. A small flat cushion or pad may also be found helpful, either in the small of the back or behind the knees. Spend a little time experimenting until the best conditions conducive to relaxation have been arranged.

When you are satisfied from your experiments that you have found the best conditions in which to be as comfortable as possible, lie on your back with your hands open and arms by your sides, but do not let them touch your body. Just let them rest comfortably at your sides, rest quietly and easily, looking at the ceiling. Don't stare, but concentrate your gaze on one spot. Don't try to do anything else. Close your eyes if it is an effort to keep them open, but do not try to "put yourself off." The object of this resting is to let your mind and body gradually slow down. If your mind starts off on some task of its own, such as making out a shopping list, or working on some problem, bring it back and remind yourself of what you are doing. After a brief interval, particularly if you have been busy previously, you will feel various tirednesses of which you were not conscious before. You will be able to feel these sensations of tiredness specifically located in various muscles in the arms, legs, hands, back, shoulders and feet.

The next step is to mentally "feel" each of these in turn.

Let yourself relax as far as you can. Then direct your attention to your right hand and let it remain there for about ten seconds, then transfer your attention to your left hand, and then to your right foot, and then to your left foot, again spending about ten seconds on each. After this,transfer your awareness to the sensations present in the muscles of the face, lips, tongue and mouth. As far as possible,avoid moving any of these parts.

You will find that when you direct your attention to one part of your body, you will forget all the other parts of your body. Go over your hands, feet and muscles in your face, as just directed,three times. You will notice as the exercise proceeds, that any tensions which may have been present when you commenced the exercise will begin to ease and die down.

A verbal description of the process of acquiring a new sensory perception must, of necessity, be inadequate. The first part of the exercise which we are now describing is directed towards recognising this feeling of tension, and becoming aware of its varying degree of strength—or, what is the same thing, to recognising the absence of tension which is, of course, the state of being relaxed.

Even if you think that your progress is excellent, devote at least three sessions to the above exercise before attempting to proceed further. Now experiment by directing your attention to different parts of your body. Progress is being made when it is found that the attention can be directed over the biceps, the muscles of the forearm, wrists, thighs, calves, ankles, feet, shoulders, back, neck and facial muscles without the mind wandering away from the task for a moment. It will be noticed after several sessions that an increasingly pleasant feeling of ease and comfort is experienced after this routine of General Relaxation. Also it will be found that restlessness has disappeared, and it is possible to stay resting immobile for longer periods without any movement.

To some, this exercise may constitute the greatest hurdle, and everything else that follows may, by comparison, seem easy. One test of having made progress is a growing awareness of the very different and distinct characters of the two sensations of relaxation and tension. A second way in which progress can be gauged is the manner in which it is possible to direct attention to the awareness of any part of the body and forget everything else.

The practice sessions should last at least five minutes and preferably should be carried out at least once a day; the longer the sessions and the more frequently they are carried out the better. The quality or standard of the general relaxation achieved will continue to improve with practice, as the effects of the work are cumulative. There is no one particular time which is best; many people find a session just before retiring produces very good results.

When you have attained some degree of familiarity with your relaxation exercises and they can be carried out more or less automatically, you are ready to take the first real step in using the self-suggestion techniques. This is by beginning to carry out daily self-suggestion sessions.

Let us revert to our example of the mind resembling a business house in which the managers—that is, the Will and Intellect (the conscious mind)—are sometimes prevented from getting messages through to the workers in the unconscious mind by a guard who acts as a kind of censor. This is the reason for the relaxing exercises as a result of which the guard can be lulled into a quiescent state, and so enable the managers to quietly pass on their messages in the form of suggestions, to the workers who are the positive elements in the unconscious mind.

Each one of us has his own pace in learning these techniques. There are very few people who can master this General Relaxation routine immediately. The average individual finds the first exercise needs a fair amount of repetition, but if he begins to make the suggestions recommended, he will benefit. Do not try to go ahead too quickly as this could defeat its own purpose, for if we try to rush matters or use force, we wake up the guardian who may stop our suggestions getting through. In other words, the more relaxed you are, the more easily will your suggestions get through to the unconscious mind.

As a general principle, the simpler the suggestions are, the better. Concentrate on making suggestions of gradual improvement. When you are relaxed mentally, repeat to yourself the suggestions recommended at the end of the paragraph. You can alter the actual wording of the suggestions as long as the meaning is unaltered, but it is advisable to have the patience to limit yourself to the general meaning of these suggestions. They serve as a foundation; once you have learned the techniques you can make all manner of suggestions, but first make sure of establishing some foundation on which to build.

"I am going to have the patience to learn this technique and mobilise all the positive elements in my make-up and get rid of my problems and troubles."

"I am going to master this technique of suggestion."

"I am going to get my unconscious mind to work for me and not against me."

CHAPTER FOUR

DIFFERENTIAL RELAXATION

When you are satisfied that a fair standard of General Relaxation has been achieved, you are ready to deliberately create local muscular tensions, so that they may be more closely examined.

Exercise No. 1

This exercise is carried out as follows:—Whilst lying relaxed, without in any way altering the position of your body, raise the right arm until, with fingers straight out, the arm is raised about six inches off the couch or floor on which you are lying. See that it is extended stiff and straight, whilst the left arm remains limp by your side. Pay particular attention to seeing that no other movements of your body, limbs or features have been made, and that, apart from the muscles involved in raising your arm, you are completely relaxed. Whilst the arm is extended, mentally note the different sensation of tension in this arm from that in the rest of the body. Switch your attention to the tense arm and then to the limp one and contrast the sensation in each.

When the character of the relaxed state of your body, as different from the tenseness of your arm, is quite plainly felt, start to increase this difference in sensation by intensifying the tension in the right arm by tensing the muscles. Keep them tense for about two to five seconds, but when this becomes slightly painful let the arm go limp and drop.

Let it rest until the sensations of tension or tiredness disappear and the feeling is replaced gradually by the pleasant feeling which comes when tension or strain is absent. Note the sensations not only in a general way, but also as they are specifically located in the fingers, the hand, forearms, in the bicep and the shoulder muscles. Repeat the exercise with the left arm whilst resting the right arm. When the different character of the sensation of relaxation and tension has consciously been identified in both arms, repeat the exercise but this time do not lift the arm. The arm should now be left lying at your side, but the muscles are to be tensed so that the feelings of tension are experienced. Then "let go" the tension and wait until the pleasant feeling of relaxation is felt. This may take some minutes. Again tense the muscles, but this time do not tense them so strongly, or for so long. Rest again until the feeling is one of relaxation, and continue to rest and feel this relaxation becoming more complete. Reinforce your efforts to relax now by using mental suggestion. Whilst mentally making suggestions, watch that you do not unconsciously start to move your lips and tongue as though you were speaking. The suggestions are to be made mentally only.

The sequence should be:

(1) Tense the muscles
(2) "Let go"
(3) Rest
(4) Note the sensations
(5) Whilst resting, use suggestions to "let go" a little more each time. The suggestions to be employed are, "My arm is becoming more relaxed," "My arm is feeling more and more relaxed each time I do this exercise." Repeat these suggestions a number of

times. Continue with suggestions which seem most helpful and most conducive to "letting go" or decreasing tension.

Remember, when you think you have relaxed to the utmost, you have not really done so. When you rest, use suggestion and tensions will subside of their own accord, providing you do not rush matters or try to get results too rapidly.

Exercise No. 2

For this exercise, lie down, relax and when completely at ease, stretch out the right leg and stiffen it. The toe should be pointed down, as though you were trying to touch something with your foot, just beyond your reach. Do not lift your leg, just stretch it, whilst letting its weight be supported by whatever you are lying on. Hold this position, until you can locate tensions separately in your thigh, calf, ankle and foot muscles. As soon as you locate them, relax and let your leg settle down under its own weight, and mentally note the difference in sensations in exactly the same way as in the previous exercise with your arms. This comparison, is, of course, purely a mental comparison. When you have rested for a short period, again tense the left leg, but this time the tension must be a little less and for a shorter period. Again rest, and notice the difference in sensations.

Exercise No. 3

For this exercise lie down and relax, then tighten or tense the muscles in the small of the back so that it is slightly arched. Hold this tension for a few seconds, and then draw in the abdominal muscles so that the stomach is pulled inwards and upwards. Hold this for a few seconds, and then relax. During the tension period the lower part of the back will be lifted clear of the support on which you are lying. Do not use a great deal of effort, no more than is necessary to raise your back about one inch. Then relax.

After this exercise has been carried out three times,the exercise of the trunk is varied by shrugging the shoulders, and after holding them hunched up for a few seconds, letting them flop relaxed. It will be found that through the attention being first directed to one group of muscles and then to another, it is possible by this means to achieve a greater degree of relaxation than was possible before you identified these groups of muscles separately. During this exercise,concentrate on the idea that all the muscles of the trunk are limp and that none are tense or taut.

Exercise No. 4

Each successive exercise adds further groups of muscles to those already relaxed. In this way relaxation already achieved becomes more complete.

When relaxed, gently let the head roll from one side to the other. Do this very slowly, letting it fall under its own weight from right to left. When the head has turned over as far as it will go in one direction, let it stay there for a while. Feel the heaviness of the facial flesh as it tends to sag. Your jaw muscles should not be clamped, but relaxed, and as a result your mouth may open slightly. Relax your tongue, which will lie flaccid in your mouth. When you have located the various sensations or sensory perceptions in your face, lips, tongue, etc, roll your head slowly over to the other side, and again note the sensations. In the periods of rest during this exercise, which should be performed very slowly, you may feel a degree of mental detachment greater than you have encountered so far.

Concentrate on relaxing the head, neck and facial muscles and aid this process by continued suggestions of relaxation.

The object of the preceding exercises is to acquire a new sensory perception. This is not easy in the beginning because the feelings or sensations are vague, indistinct and some are not in clearly defined areas, until some practice has been carried out. The sensations become clearer and more definite with continued practice. The general attitude of mind in performing the exercises should be to take it easy, with no attempt to hurry or rush. They are to be performed physically in an easy going, languid manner, but mentally remaining fully attentive. In the tensing movements use very little effort, the less the better. The object of the exercises is not physical exercise, but the reverse.

It will be clear that the relaxation exercises are a means of quietening and slowing down the mental and emotional activities so that messages can be passed quietly into the unconscious mind.

When we relax and shut our eyes we tend to drift towards a sleep or trance state, that is if we do not keep the mind switched on. Do not think you must go into a deep trance to get suggestions through to your unconscious mind. This is not so. Your suggestions will get through even if you have attained only the lightest of trances. It is true that you may have to patiently repeat the suggestions daily, but the main point is that you successfully deal with your problems, so even if your trance state is not as deep as you wish, this will not prevent you successfully using self-suggestion.

Some people achieve their objectives without ever experiencing the trance state, so do not hold up your progress by waiting until you have achieved some preconceived idea of what the trance state should be. During each suggestion session make the following suggestions to yourself:

"I am going to deal conclusively with my problems once and for all."

"I will have the patience and the perseverance to keep on practising."

CHAPTER FIVE

ROUTINE OF SELF-SUGGESTION SESSION

In the preceding sections we have so far been concerned with certain instructions for relaxation routines and the suggestions given at the end of sections Three and Four.

Now you are ready for the next step. Having relaxed, lie down with your eyes closed and, under closed eyelids direct your eyes slightly upwards as though you were looking at a spot between your eyebrows. It may be found helpful to place a small object (a coin will do), in the centre of the forehead on which to concentrate. Whilst doing this the eyes must remain closed. Do not strain, but keep them directed in that position until it becomes an effort to do so. If you feel any strain or effort in maintaining this position of the eyes, just "let go" and rest. Don't do anything at all. Do not open your eyes. Don't bother to think about your eyes, they may move under your lids or they may not. If they want to move, let them. If they want to stay as they are, let them. Many people at this stage feel very detached. With continued practice, the feeling of detachment becomes deeper.

Do not let your mind begin analysing or reflecting on how you are progressing with your exercises while you are engaged in carrying them out.

Just launch yourself into the routine and submit or surrender yourself to the languid feeling which will result from carrying out the exercises.

You may begin to experience some degree of light trance at this stage, but the majority of people have to continue with further methods to heighten the state of suggestibility. Begin each session by relaxing and you will notice now, having carried out a daily practice session for a few weeks, you are able to achieve the relaxed state more rapidly. You will now be able to leave out the detailed attention to the arms, legs, etc.

As the next step in learning self-suggestion and auto-hypnosis, the following method is in my opinion a sound basic method to which you can add any variations you will later find helpful.

One, two, three, Method. This method can be used anywhere, any time. No preparation is required and there is no need to isolate oneself. On the lines described later in this section, it may be practised in a restaurant, sitting in a bus, or during a few minutes at business. To describe this as a method seems over-elaborate, for once the ability "to sink into oneself" has been mastered, all that is necessary is the simple routine which follows. Take a few deep breaths, fix the eyes on some object such as an electric light switch or a door knob, and count "one, two, three" and at three let your eyes gently close. Continue counting softly to yourself up to "ten." When you get to "ten," direct your attention to your right thumb and mentally count again to ten, then transfer your attention to the first finger of your right hand and again count to "ten," then to the second finger and so with all the fingers on both hands. Count slowly and silently at a speed which does not leave time for other thoughts to break in whilst counting.

Take your time over the ritual of counting your fingers and when this is completed, direct your attention to your mouth and sense the feeling of your lips and tongue. It will help to locate this feeling if you slightly move your tongue. Following this, direct your attention inwards as though to the spot between your eyes mentioned in the previous method.

Whilst you have been practising, subtle mental and physical changes will have been taking place quite automatically. If, for example, you were counting at the rate of one each second, by the time you had brought your awareness to the spot between your eyes, about two minutes would have passed since you began, and during that time with your eyes shut and your attention focused at a sensory level of awareness by the monotony of counting, a slow but subtle drift towards the trance state will have occurred.

Up till now you have had to isolate yourself to carry out your practice. Now you can take a big step forward by relaxing and administering suggestions to yourself wherever you may be.

In the previous exercises of relaxing your arms, legs, back, you have been practising differential relaxation, that is, the relaxing of all muscles other than those actually necessary for the performance of any particular task. This ability is now applied to relaxing *while seated in a chair*. The object of being able to carry out the General Relaxation exercise *while seated* is so that relaxation can be practised at any time without the necessity of lying down. Once general relaxation has been mastered while seated, it is possible to carry out self-suggestion, on a train or bus, or wherever you may be, without anyone being aware of what you are doing.

If you intend carrying out self-suggestion whilst seated, again go through the exercises of tensing the arms, tensing the legs and head lolling *whilst you are sitting*. Do this until you experience the same sensation of heaviness and relaxation which you have had whilst lying down.

This differential functioning can be performed, not only

by our muscles, but also by consciousness itself. A very good example is furnished by our hearing which is highly selective. It selects from the medley of sound in everyday life only those which, in some way, require our attention. Many noises, such as those of cars, clocks, voices, etc., are allowed to pass unnoticed without being brought to our conscious attention for the simple reason they are of no concern or interest to us.

After a few sessions the sensory appreciation of tension will be more clearly defined, and the ability to consciously "let go," physically and mentally, comes more under conscious control. Repeat each exercise until you are satisfied that you have made some progress, but do not expect anything dramatic or startling; just keep on producing the maximum feeling of detachment, ease and relaxation that you can. The effects of these exercises are cumulative, and the degree of detachment which is attained is determined mainly by the regularity with which the exercises are carried out, and the absence of any *negative* self-suggestion during or in between practice sessions.

At each session when you have carried out your relaxation routine, let the suggestions with which this chapter ends float through your mind. In relaxing you have been preparing your body, and now with suggestions of this nature, you are mobilising inner resources which will aid you.

Profiting by Arjuna's experience, you can hasten your acquisition of the superior weapons (or techniques) which will enable you to conclusively deal with your problems by patiently plodding away on your daily suggestion sessions. You can get through from day to day with the weapons you have, but to win conclusively you may want superior weapons. These weapons (like Arjuna) you can acquire by asking for aid from the positive elements in your unconscious mind by suggestions of the following nature:

"One way or another I am going to get rid of my trouble/complaint/ailment" (mentioning whatever your objective may be).

"If it is necessary for me to gain further knowledge, I want my unconscious mind to work for me and help me to discover this knowledge."

"I am willing if necessary to change my methods . . . all I want to do is to solve my problem."

"With all my heart and soul I sincerely want to get rid of this problem once and for all and want all the help I can get."

Your work so far could be likened to preparing the ground and in the next chapter we will begin to examine and choose the seeds (or suggestions) we wish to plant.

CHAPTER SIX

DEVISING THE RIGHT SUGGESTIONS

We will now consider how we can plan and devise more informed suggestions to pass on to the positive elements in our unconscious mind.

Most people beginning to learn self-hypnosis are sure they know what suggestions they wish to make . . . in most cases they are wrong. They know what they wish to achieve, but very few know the best suggestions to use to bring about what they desire. At the beginning of this Course I told the story of how Arjuna received unexpected help, and how by making suggestions similar to those I prescribed at the end of the last Session, unexpected aid will come from the unconscious mind. If we enlist its aid it will show us opportunities we have not previously seen; it will show us hidden obstacles and how they can be avoided; it will show us how to alter our attitude towards unalterable circumstances; it will quicken hope, free enthusiasms, and inspire us, but we must not, like Arjuna, let courage make us so cocksure that we think we can order the unconscious mind about. This cannot be done—but we can get its co-operation.

An excellent example of a good strategetical approach in using suggestion techniques was the case of a man who, although he never achieved any real depth of trance, cured himself of nervous tensions, fears, indifferent health, poor memory, and gained promotion. He had been employed for many years as a clerk, though his knowledge and experience of the business fitted him for a far better position. Following the instructions in the Course, he began by employing suggestions on the following lines—"I am going to use my abilities to the full, I am not going to be a slave to ill health, I am going to rid myself of whatever it is that holds me back. I am going to lose this nervousness. I want the courage to see if I am creating difficulties for myself. If I am, I will find some way of dealing with them. I am going to get on at my work." He carried on with these suggestions for some days. Then one night he had a strange dream. He dreamed that one of the Directors of his business was coming towards him with a check in his hand, and he, the dreamer, turned and ran away from this Director, feeling very much afraid. Then he began to notice that at business he was very tense whenever this Director came into the office. He began to realise that unconsciously he was very much afraid of this Director and that this was the underlying reason for his mediocre performance at business. Unconsciously he was avoiding responsibility and promotion which would have brought him under this Director's immediate supervision. He continued with his suggestions and soon discovered that the Director's appearance was reminiscent of a school teacher who had bullied him unmercifully at school. Once the hidden cause of his tensions and fears came to consciousness, he began to see the nature of the conflict and how he had previously been fighting to repress his fears and tensions. Once he saw the real underlying cause of his difficulties, he carried on with self-diagnostic suggestions, and day by day the energies which had been absorbed by the repressed fears were freed. He felt strangely relieved, and his suggestions "I know I can do a better job" had a ring of truth which would not have been the case had he begun with parrotlike suggestions of, "I have 100 per cent confidence." If he had used short-sighted suggestion he would have repressed his fears and would have been fighting his unconscious mind instead of getting its co-operation. As will be seen in this example, the all important point is to gain the co-operation of the unconscious mind, by choosing the right suggestions and, if necessary, altering them.

Do not try to rush matters. If results are going to come quickly, nothing will stop them, but to build up hopes of results immediately leaves one open to disappointment. The strategy I recommend is that the individual say to himself: "I will do my best to keep up regular practice. If I can only improve one per cent a day I will not grumble, but I am going to get the co-operation of my unconscious mind as soon as I can. One thing is certain, I am going to deal with this (stating own problem). I am going to go on with it until I succeed and the job is finished." By adopting this attitude, emotional ups and downs will be avoided, and in consequence, more rapid progress made.

Another important point in planning is to remember that we do not consciously invent or make up the suggestions. It is true we become aware of them in our conscious minds. But the desires for peace of mind, health and happiness all spring from the unconscious mind. They are the desires of the unconscious and if it is approached with sincerity and patience it will allow man to tap energies he never dreamed he possessed, carry out feats which seemed impossible and cure complaints which had been regarded as hopeless.

By becoming conscious of the contradictory impulses from within, and the influences from the outside world, and selecting and strengthening those which will enable us to achieve what we want, the power to control ourselves is acquired. We are enabled to achieve these desired changes in ourselves because we can create, for a short time, the mental images and thoughts of the things we wish to achieve. In this way we can alter our lives by building new habits and attitudes, and thus re-direct the elemental energy of the instincts to the purposes of the will.

In life, until a man has achieved some knowledge of self, he stands at a crossroad. Ahead of him lie two divergent roads. One leads to all the things he fears and dreads, whilst the other is the road by which he can reach his ideals, his hopes and his higher aspirations. This is what Freud meant when he said that each man could reach heights he had never dreamt of, and could fall to depths he had never imagined. The framing of a man's suggestions are chosen from the things that he hopes, wishes and desires, and as soon as he begins consciously and consistently to practise self-suggestions he begins to move positively and with certainty towards the things he most desires, and to leave his fears behind him.

Suggestions in the beginning can be of a very general nature. All that is necessary is that they are sincere, and the more simple and uncomplicated the better. A number of specimen suggestions are now given. They begin with suggestions which are designed to strengthen the resolution of the individual to continue the task he has begun in studying this Course, and to achieve his objectives.

"I will remember to carry out my exercises."

"I will make steady progress."

"I want to become more and more enthusiastic about altering my life."

"Every time I read or practise I will do my very best to make progress."

"I am willing to make whatever changes may be necessary in my life to attain what I desire."

"Each day I will work to be more self-possessed and surer of myself."

"I want to get a bird's eye view of my life and see what is essential to my happiness and success."

"I will observe and be pleased with my successes, and I will learn from any setbacks."

"I will alter what is within my power to alter, and will change my attitude towards those things which I cannot change."

"My patience will increase every day, and things that used to disturb me will leave me unmoved."

"I shall not talk, think, or let my mind dwell on unpleasant, morbid subjects."

"I shall direct my thoughts towards pleasant things, and the sort of individual I should like to be."

"I shall be on my guard against what I know to be my weaknesses."

"I will see my past mistakes and try to avoid repeating them in the future."

"I will begin to see more clearly the obstacles which are preventing me from obtaining happiness, health and peace of mind, and how they may be overcome."

"If I suffer any disappointments or reverses, this will not shake my faith in myself, or in the power of suggestion."

"I am going to be able to concentrate and to think more clearly."

"I am going to be able to remember things more easily. My memory will be more retentive."

"My self-control and self-possession and confidence is going to grow steadily."

"I am going to develop mental poise, and peace of mind."

"My ability to control my mental and emotional life is growing."

"I am going to enjoy better health and have more energy."

"Every day I will observe myself and every day I will try to learn something."

"I am going to be less tense and find it easier to relax."

"I am going to be more tolerant with other people, and try to understand their difficulties."

Take your own particular desires, disabilities or difficulties and express them in words. If, for example, you lack confidence say "I am going to get over these feelings. I am going to feel more confident every day. These suggestions will help to make me stronger and have more self-control. I am not going to worry what other people think about me," and continue on these lines.

It will be noticed that many of the above suggestions refer to the future, such as: "I am going to feel more confident." This method of self-suggestion employs the phenomena of post-hypnotic suggestion which, as readers who have witnessed a hypnotic demonstration, or who have read on the subject will know, is a form of delayed action suggestion. It operates by registering impressions directly on the subconscious mind, and they are carried out at a later date. The most common example of self administered post-hypnotic suggestion is when someone says to himself: "Tomorrow morning *I am going to wake up* at seven o'clock." If he does wake up at seven o'clock he has succeeded in giving himself a post-hypnotic suggestion. The ability to do this is an inherent faculty in everyone and it can be employed to alter one's future attitude, actions or thoughts and by this means many changes can be effected which cannot be effected by will power alone.

It cannot be over-emphasised that self-suggestion and

self-hypnotism are a means to an end, and the suggestions must be sound and reasonable and planned on a long-term policy if real lasting benefit is to follow. The majority of nervous breakdowns occur because people have success-fully suggested to themselves that they were capable of greater efforts than they were in reality able to carry out. They had used suggestion to stifle the warnings of their fatigue centres and drawn recklessly on their reserves of nervous energy until they collapsed. This is obviously not an intelligent use of self-suggestion. It is necessary that the suggestions made to oneself should not make undue demands on one's body, but rather that they should aid the body through suggestions of sound sleep, alterations in diet, lowering of tensions, and intelligent direction of effort which will enable the body to work more efficiently.

The mistake of using the power of suggestion without carefully considering the nature of the suggestions made can be exemplified by the following story:—A hypnotist met a man who was very worried and asked why he looked so worried. The man replied: "I am very worried about my overdraft at the bank, it kept me awake last night and I can't bear the idea of spending any money." The hypno-tist said: "I'll soon fix that—sit down and relax." He then hypnotised the man and proceeded to give suggestions on the following lines: "You will forget all about your bank manager and all about your overdraft. When you wake up all your money troubles will have vanished. If you see anything in a shop which you want, you'll go right in and buy it." Everyone will see the fallacy of symptom removal in such a case, but it should be kept in mind that the same laws apply whether we are spending money or nervous energy for, in both cases, overdrafts cannot be indefinitely increased.

It was previously commented on that the things that we

wish to achieve are inherent strivings, or the expression of the deepest aspirations of one's nature. The suggestions prepared by one sincerely desiring to establish his life on a sound basis, to help others, and to achieve peace of mind, is almost identical with prayers which are also addressed to the source of all life. This similarity is clearly seen in one of the prayers of St. Francis of Assisi which follows:

Lord make me an instrument of thy peace
Where there is hatred—let me sow love
Where there is doubt—let me sow faith
Where there is despair—let me sow hope
Where there is darkness—light
Where there is sadness—joy
O Divine Master grant that I do not so much seek
    to be consoled as to console—
    to be understood as to understand—
    to be loved as to love.
For it is in giving that we receive—
    in pardoning that we are pardoned—
    and in dying that we are born to everlasting
    life.

Self-treatment suggestions aimed at achieving normal, healthy functioning of the mind, body, and emotions are not alien demands imposed from outside. They are the conscious expression of inherent desires from within. Unconscious activities superintend the electro-chemical transformation of food and energy and the functions of repairing and replacing broken or injured skin, bone and tissue. In short, all the unconscious processes strive to correct mal-functioning of all kinds, and to maintain or regain health. This process can be assisted by conscious suggestions. One of the most important factors in success-ful suggestions is the clear interpretation of these inherent strivings, the fusion of the conscious with the unconscious. This is the recognition of the healthy and constructive aims of the unconscious and their reinforcement by the conscious mind; this and the removal or circumvention of the resistances to this process are the main factors in successful suggestion. Self-doubt, and forgetting to carry out regular suggestion sessions,are the main obstacles.

In framing suggestions it is wisest, particularly in the initial stages, not to expect too much. Set a modest pro-gramme. If a difficulty has existed for some time, in all probability attempts to treat it will have already been made unsuccessfully. If this is so, the individual will, despite himself, have entertained negative suggestions. They can, however, be outweighed by regular positive suggestions. No one knows better than the individual himself his hopes and fears, the ways in which he desires to alter his life, and some of the circumstances which help and some of those which hinder him. Frame the sugges-tions of what you wish to accomplish. These desires should be expressed in clear, short, easily understood sentences.

Some of these suggestions will be of a personal nature, designed to fulfil your needs. They will probably deal with many aspects of your life such as diet, sleep, sex or per-sonal habits, intimate associations with others, future plans, and matters with which no one but you yourself are acquainted.

In the next chapter we will deal with self-observation which enables you to see and follow up the clues and guidance offered to you by your unconscious mind.

CHAPTER SEVEN

SELF-OBSERVATION BETWEEN SUGGESTION SESSIONS

Self- observation means observing the way in which our suggestions have affected our behaviour. This self-observation calls for frank self-scrutiny, but is carried out solely for the purpose of discovering our mistakes so that we may avoid or overcome them.

Watch for the negative moods in yourself. When in these moods,the most profitable observations can be made. For example, if a thought such as, "I am not making sufficient progress," occurs, do not repress it, do not conceal your doubts from yourself. Suggestion can rid you of them but you cannot put anything right until you know what it is that is wrong. Self-honesty is necessary in observing oneself. It is no good attempting to concentrate on the bright side, and to pretend that the dark side does not exist. Repression is permissible as a temporary expedient and, in many cases, is a necessary measure to free our minds to carry on our everyday occupation, but, as a permanent policy it is disastrous for it succeeds only when our energy level is sufficiently high to inhibit or repress the unwanted thoughts, emotions and compulsions. Self-observation or the observing of other people gives ample proof that until an individual has arrived at a certain stage in development, self-control is lessened through shocks, fatigue,and illness. Courage, endurance and will power are needed to repress difficulties, doubts and fears, but courage of a different order is required to be frank with ourselves, and to admit our limitations. It might appear that to admit one's limitations, doubts and fears, would cause one to lose ground, but in actual fact through frank admission of our limitations comes strength of a new order. We no longer make impossible demands upon ourselves. We can afford to take reverses. It is no longer a question to "do or die." A negative mood, a shock or some reverse is an episode and not a major defeat once one acquires this wider and more flexible strategy. When we gain a more realistic appraisal of our strengths and weaknesses, we can extend a new tolerance to ourselves and to others (for we cannot be kind to others until we can be kind to ourselves). With this alteration in our attitude we can view our shortcomings, with tolerance, for criticism must be kind to be constructive.

In observing oneself whilst carrying on the day's work, note the incidents which affect you adversely, whether they be people, your own thoughts, actions, foods, incidents or any other circumstances. A sound method is to write down the next two incidents which annoy or irritate you, the next two which make you sad, the next two which create tension, the next two which make you feel pleased with yourself. If something causes you to be tense, afraid, annoyed, pleased, reflect and ask yourself questions about this reaction. "Why did I feel like that?" "At whom, or at what, was the feeling directed?" "What caused the emotion or physical disturbance?" These reactions reveal the hidden character structure which can only be learned by these devious approaches. Self-observation is strictly practical work which can be aided by asking oneself questions such as: "What is the biggest mistake I have made today?" "What have I learned today?" etc.

In watching for results from the suggestions you have given yourself, it is important to remember that there is frequently a time lag between suggestions being given and their fulfilment. Sometimes it is necessary to continue suggestions for some time before their effects are noticed, for frequently inner resistances have to be overcome. If it were not for this fact all suggestions, both good and bad, would become immediately effective.

Be on your guard for a short time after having success-fully achieved a change in habit. In an unguarded moment, before the new habit has become firmly estab-lished, it is easy to slide back. Carry on with your sugges-tions for a few days in order to consolidate the position. For example, if someone, through suggestion, had given up smoking, it would be wise for a few days to continue to suggest: "I have given up smoking and *will not* smoke again. I will *not be* caught off my guard when someone offers me a cigarette. I *will not* be talked into smoking," etc.

The purpose of observing oneself is to note the changes which you have effected in yourself as a result of your self-suggestions. Note the improvements and benefits you have achieved, as these evidences of successful self-suggestion make further advances easier and also consolidate the im-provements made and bed them down into permanent habits. Where your self-suggestions have not met with the success you anticipated, do not let this discourage you. The technique of suggestion is something to be learned, and is one in which the beginner, as in any other subject will have failures. Where there are failures, change the type of suggestion, approach your objective from another angle.

The intelligent application of self-suggestion calls for careful thought and constant revision of suggestions. It is a means to an end. You are the only one who knows the particular difficulties and problems with which you are faced, the disabilities, habits and attitudes of which you wish to rid yourself, and the life you desire to live in the future. To attain these ends it may be necessary for you to frequently reshape your suggestions, guided by what is learned during self-observation.

As a result of self-observation some people find that they have not the time to carry out exercises. Others find that they forget to carry them out. If these obstacles arise— then some action should be taken. It is only by facing facts that we can alter ourselves. It must not be forgotten that the majority of resolutions that people make are forgotten, for the line of least resistance is to do today what we did yesterday, and most likely we will do the same tomorrow. Habits are strong, and some persistence in effort is necessary if we are to effect changes in ourselves. If you should suddenly realise that you have forgotten to carry out an exercise or something you had planned, close your eyes and mentally repeat, very rapidly, to yourself: "I will not forget . . . I will not forget . . . I will not forget." Spend a minute or two doing this. It is also a very sound idea to fall back on mechanical reminders, such as carrying round written instructions to oneself, or to carry out waking suggestions at certain times,—before every meal, when you get up, before going to sleep, every time the sun goes down, or, if you are indoors, when the lights are switched on. Two minutes waking suggestion three or four times a day will effect a great deal of influence on one's life if one is sincere in desiring what one asks for. Obviously, suggestions would, in cases of forgetfulness, be directed towards curing this shortcoming which could, if allowed to go unchecked, bring your efforts to effect alterations in yourself through this course to a standstill. In cases such as this, suggestions would be on the following lines: "I am not going to forget," "I will remember more easily in future." "From now on I shall do my practice more regularly."

If your self-suggestion has for a while been progressing well and you seem to come to a standstill, or to have setbacks, there will be reasons for this. Try to find them out. It may be caused by a chill, a slight indisposition, the result of unusual physical or mental efforts, a disruption of one's affairs, or some temporary disturbances. These changes may produce temporary setbacks, and should be taken into account. Planned suggestions directed specifically towards them can do much to ameliorate or offset these disturbances. Sometimes people encounter setbacks because they attempt to progress too rapidly, and if the individual tries to force himself, or to progress too rapidly, unconscious resistances may come into operation. The changes which are being produced by suggestion are a natural process, and the time taken to effect them varies according to the difficulties, inner resistances, strength of existing habits, and particular circumstances in the life of each individual. The golden rule in suggestion technique is NO FORCING. Gentle persistence is the keynote.

If something disturbs or upsets you during the day, take what practical action you can to deal with the incident and its possible consequences. To prevent its repetition, put the matter from your mind; suggestions dealing with the matter can be framed later when you are replanning your suggestions. To banish difficulties from one's mind consciously is not necessarily a harmful repression, for, in other words, there are "permissible repressions."

Whatever progress you make with trance induction, at every opportunity use waking suggestions, as the object of the self-suggestion techniques is not to conduct one's life by carrying out a series of post-hypnotic suggestions, but by the integration of the unconscious activities with the conscious, intellectual activities.

Remarkable though the powers of Self-Suggestion and Self Hypnotism may be, they are powerless to alter many conditions of life. They cannot bring back our youth, or those we have lost, nor can they make good irreparable physical damage, but through these powers of self-suggestion we can rise above the inevitable changes that are caused by the passing of time BY ALTERING OUR ATTITUDE TOWARDS THOSE CIRCUMSTANCES WHICH WE ARE POWERLESS TO CHANGE.

We have so far dealt with a method of relaxation and the first steps in self-suggestion. These two techniques are combined in the self-suggestion session which you are now carrying out. Later we will be dealing with more advanced methods of trance induction, but first we must give some attention to the way in which we register suggestions in the unconscious mind.

CHAPTER EIGHT

REGISTERING SUGGESTIONS IN THE UNCONSCIOUS MIND

There are certain basic desires in everyone which strive for self-expression. If they remain unexpressed the individual becomes frustrated, for his life force is strangled back. It is here suggested that these desires, whether they be a desire for better health, more confidence, more friends, success in some undertaking, or the ability to help others, should be expressed and made articulate in the form of suggestions. Throughout the ages people have striven in various ways to express their inner needs. They have wished, hoped, prayed and used self-suggestion, and the more simply and sincerely they have been able to do so, the more successfully have their wishes come to fruition.

Registering suggestions in the unconscious mind actually requires very little effort ... if the preparatory work on relaxation has been done and what you are going to suggest has been previously decided.

Having isolated yourself from the outside world and directed the attention inwards, allow yourself to mentally drift away from the world of sight and sound into an inner world. In a dreamy, detached fashion carry out the trance induction routine of counting, and noting the heaviness of the body and other sensations of detachment. This should go on automatically. There is a complete submission to the sensation of drifting and to effortlessly repeating silently to oneself, "I am sinking down . . . further . . . further" (or whatever formula you are using). Surrender to this experience. Reason is stilled and becomes a silent spectator to this feeling and experience of floating detachment.

Gradually this sensation of sinking will come to a point where it seems to stop and one remains stationary . . . poised as it were, vaguely aware, but with nothing happening. This is just as it should be . . . the will, present but not being exercised. Rather like a shepherd, who, effortlessly resting on the hillside, sees all the movements of his flock and his awareness is in the role of a passive witness. This is approaching the borderland separating the conscious from the unconscious mind, to go beyond this point means that control would be lost. This is the point when suggestions will be registered in the unconscious mind. This is achieved by letting your suggestions float through your mind.

Exercises in the Course to create this state can be likened to the tilling of the ground . . . and the act of registering self-suggestions, to the planting of seeds. If the ground has been well tilled, i.e., if the relaxation exercises have been carried out, and the formulation or reflection on suggestions also carried out, the registering of the desired instructions upon the unconscious mind will not be difficult. It is essential that no effort is exerted when making self-suggestions. If the judgment begins analysing what is occurring, the process of registering ideas in the unconscious mind is immediately brought to a standstill. It is as though, after planting seeds the gardener were to dig up the tiny, fragile seedlings to see how they are growing. The result would probably be to destroy the plants before they had time to establish themselves. It is the absence of any intellectual interference, which enables suggestions to take root in the unconscious mind. The success of suggestion is dependent on by-passing the conscious mind and registering the desired impression directly on the unconscious mind.

If we are sufficiently absorbed in anything we forget everything else and become completely immersed in it. No effort is necessary to give attention to an interesting book, a TV, or radio program. It holds our whole attention.

Many people feel that they cannot give the same sustained attention to carrying out exercises on relaxation, trance induction, and self-suggestions as they would to an interesting book or film. Concentration is largely a matter of interest, but what would the man who feels he cannot concentrate reply if he were asked: "ARE YOU INTERESTED IN FEELING PHYSICALLY AND MENTALLY FIT? ARE YOU INTERESTED IN LEAVING ALL YOUR TROUBLES AND DIFFICULTIES BEHIND YOU?" Not only will he be interested, but as soon as he can see a practical way of achieving fitness and freedom from worry, he will do all he can to attain them.

Waking suggestions are carried out by repetition and can be made to oneself at any time. It does not matter where you are: standing, walking, or sitting, once the technique is grasped, it is no longer necessary to isolate oneself. In the beginning it is necessary to have the most favourable conditions, but later all this is unnecessary. Many people who have mastered self-suggestion never go into a trance to register suggestions in their minds. All they do is close their eyes and register the desired suggestion. It would have value if the reader pauses at the end of this paragraph and says to himself (and means it) " I *am* going to learn how to get more control over my mind . . . I *am* going to do this."

It is a good practice to carry out waking suggestions

regularly by setting a fixed time for making them to oneself. For example, every lunch time set aside a few minutes. Similarly use as a cue, or reminder, some happening such as when the electric light goes on, or when you glance at your watch, and at each of these times give yourself a few waking suggestions. All that is necessary is to close your eyes and count three and impress the suggestion on your mind, open your eyes and carry on with whatever you were doing. The more often you do this, the more effectively your suggestions will be registered.

Some people repeat waking suggestions to themselves over and over again as they lie in bed before going to sleep. One method of self-suggestion is to write down suggestions on a piece of paper, and last thing at night read it ten times, then place the paper under the pillow and sleep on it. Another is to write out suggestions for the day, and carry them around in one's pocket. It is a good idea to write out the week's suggestions in one's diary. It is also a useful device to write out suggestions in the form of a letter and post it to oneself and when receiving it to read and re-read several times.

Implanting suggestions in the mind is like planting seeds in a garden. Just as it is necessary to keep a garden clear of weeds, it is in a similar fashion necessary to keep the mind clear of negative thoughts.

Do not always repress doubts, try to trace what has caused them, to see if they arise from some matter which requires your attention.

Before turning to the next chapter, let us pause to review the method employed in this course. It is not advocated that you should relax and repeat the same suggestions every day. Once the method is grasped you will find it becomes interwoven into all your thinking, wishing, and planning. This does not mean you will be day-dreaming or suggesting to yourself all day, but it does mean a new kind of informed awareness in thinking about yourself, your plans, and in observing yourself and other people; and instead of chance or negative reactions, you will find you have positive reactions which are the result of your following a programme.

The programme is as follows:

PLANNING
SUGGESTIBLE STATE (creation of)
REGISTERING SUGGESTIONS IN UNCONSCIOUS MIND
SELF-OBSERVATION
REPLANNING SUGGESTIONS

Some of these different phases, though described separately, are performed simultaneously. They are not as easy to separate in practice as they are in theory; for example, the deepening of the trance state, and the self-administration of suggestions are sometimes carried out at the same time. Also, Self-Observation and the Replanning of Suggestions will often be more or less part of the same act.

The system of self-suggestion is a program in which positive thoughts are guided and monitored towards making definite changes in one's life, instead of drifting or letting chance or the past determine what happens. The whole cycle is ceaselessly repeated . . . Planning, Suggestion Sessions, Self-Observation, Amending of, or adding to Suggestions.

CHAPTER NINE

THE SELF-HYPNOTIC TRANCE

The creation of the self-hypnotic state has been a practice since the earliest times. In most esoteric writings the importance of self-induced trances has been stressed as a method of curing ills and gaining knowledge.

Much of the work in Yoga is concerned in ultimately being able to enter a self-induced trance. This is preceded by purification of the body, inside and out, by maintaining physical postures (asanas), by breathing exercises (pranayama), and by mental concentration. In the Bhagavad Gita, Chapter 5, verses 27 and 28, is the following instruction:

"Shutting out all external objects, fixing the vision between the eyebrows, making even, the inward and outward breaths, moving between the nostrils, the sage who has controlled the senses, the mind and understanding. . . ."

Trance states are self-induced by many people all over the world. Some believe that they are making contact with Gods, or with their ancestors' spirits, or that it is a form of magic. In the West, self-hypnosis is being increasingly regarded in a much more factual way, namely as a method of contacting the unconscious mind.

Although the basic principles underlying the techniques of self-hypnotism and successful trance induction are the same in any part of the world, local conditions are not, and these make a great deal of difference to trance induction. The mental state is dependent on the chemistry of the body. Too much oxygen makes us lose control of ourselves, and with too little we become insensible. Altitude is also a real factor. In Johannesburg, at 6,000 feet above sea level, motor cars from lower altitudes need a carburettor adjustment. When we find the gross mechanism of a car can be affected by the altitude, it is not surprising that the chemistry of the body and the mental operations can also be affected. Mountains and deserts are traditional places of retreat for meditational purposes. From my experience the greater the altitude, the easier the trance induction, and this I believe is something quite apart from the amount of oxygen in the air. Some people enter a trance more easily when they have less than average oxygen in their bloodstream, and others succeed more easily when they have more than the average amount of oxygen. This is a matter which the reader must find out for himself. Before practice sessions I would recommend trying very shallow breathing for a minute before carrying out practice in your relaxation or trance induction. Then at another time try deep breathing. In subsequent sessions use deep breathing or shallow breathing, whichever suits you best.

The variations between individuals and their own local conditions make it impossible to lay down any hard and fast instructions to suit everyone.

There are many states of consciousness, but the average individual has probably not considered such a matter. It is not as though man is either awake or asleep, or that he is either conscious or unconscious. There is no such simple division. There are many intermediate states and, in fact, when we are asleep we are not really unconscious. For example, if someone were to break a window in a room in which the reader was sleeping he would wake up with a start, and in his sleep he would have heard the tinkle of the broken glass ... and yet he was asleep when the window was broken. Actually he was not completely unconscious. A part of the mind remains on duty as a sentinel even when we are asleep. If there is anything unusual, a sound, or a smell of burning, the sentinel will wake us. There are a number of these different trance states which can be cultivated. In some,the will is in abeyance but can be brought into operation to register the suggestions we wish in the unconscious mind. These states are difficult to describe, but if the reader will carry out the instructions and will co-operate by experimenting to find the best methods, he will soon discover that in this way he can gain a vastly increased control over himself.

There are various methods of increasing suggestibility and of hypnotising oneself. The most commonly used method is the Fixed Gaze, of which there are a number of variations, some of which are described in the following chapter.

It is advisable when beginning to put into operation the methods which follow, not to hold up progress by comparing the feelings you will experience with preconceived ideas about "going off." If a bowl of jelly is shaken at intervals while it is setting, and at each shaking the comment is made: "It doesn't look as if it is going to set," under these circumstances the jelly is very unlikely to ever set. Similarly with suggestion—if while carrying out exercises you are also mentally making a running commentary, progress is likely to be delayed.

The state of suggestibility differs with different people. Do not set the condition that you must go into a trance at once. There's only one way to judge the results of suggestion and that is by results. There is an Eastern proverb: "Drop by drop the pitcher is filled." No suggestions, or prayers,or good efforts are ever lost. Although you may not see dramatic results from your suggestion sessions immediately, even if you create only the lightest of trances or were only relaxing and using auto-suggestion, some of your suggestions will register in your unconscious mind where they will become an accumulating force.

It is sound strategy to say to yourself: "I am in no hurry about this. I am not going to prejudice the whole under-taking by setting a date when I should go into a trance, or when I should achieve what I want." You are an indi-vidual and every individual is different. You may achieve what you want easily and rapidly, or you may have a diffi-culty of long standing which may take some time to deal with. Do not set any time limit. Simply devote what time you can to practice, even if it is only a few minutes a day, and steadily go ahead on the lines suggested.

In many cases people write and tell me that they have achieved what they want without any appreciable depth of trance. They merely followed the instructions, making self-suggestions on the lines advocated in the Course during relaxation sessions.

Once you have acquired the art of putting suggestion into the unconscious mind it is, in fact, not necessary to lie down and go through the relaxation routine before making suggestions to yourself. Successful self-suggestion can be carried out while walking, standing, in a car or bus, or wherever you may be. When you have mastered the art of self-suggestion you can give your unconscious mind a directive, or order, without going into a trance, simply by closing your eyes for a few moments and mentally speaking to yourself. When you come to carry out the Trance Induction methods, choose one which appeals to you and begin to experiment with it. Then try others if you wish. The methods may be tried in any order. If the first one suits you, there is no need to try any of the others.

I recommend the reader to experiment—to make alterations and create the best possible conditions for himself according to his personal idiosyncrasies, the time he has available, and his environmental circumstances.

Before beginning your suggestion sessions, make arrangements for your comfort as already described. Pay particular attention to the temperature of the room and see that you will not be cold and there are no draughts . . . later on these precautions are unnecessary. Before you actually begin, start off with waking suggestions. Say to yourself, either aloud or mentally, "I am going to begin hypnotising myself." The reason for using the word "begin" is because you may not succeed at once and you are guarding yourself against disappointment by avoiding making an issue of success in a single session. If for any reason you do not wish to hypnotise yourself but wish to master the art of successful self-suggestion, say "I am going to increase my suggestibility to the utmost without letting myself go into a trance."

These preliminary waking suggestions should be directives for pre-determining your attitude during the suggestion session. The waking suggestions you should give, should be instructions suited to the circumstances and practical arrangements for your session. For example, "I am going to spend X minutes and will let myself drift off as far as possible . . . I will not criticise my efforts. If there are any interruptions, telephone calls, if someone knocks on the door or calls me, I will immediately rouse myself and will become fully alert."

In the next chapter, various methods of trance induction are described.

CHAPTER TEN

INDUCING THE SELF-HYPNOTIC TRANCE

This is a method of inducing self-hypnosis by fixing the gaze on some object, a door knob or a light switch, a candle or lamp. If using electric light, the possibility of damage to the eyes should be avoided by using a low-wattage bulb, or shading the light. The procedure to be followed is to sit some six to ten feet from the object, candle or light and to relax physically—on the lines of the relaxation previously given—and direct one's gaze upon the object or light. Gaze steadily at the spot—let the image of what you are looking at register on your mind, and continue to look at it steadily. Disregard all ideas and sensations which may present themselves, such as noises, awareness of your own breathing, etc. You will become aware that your body is becoming heavier, and that you are becoming drowsier, and that your eyes will feel as though they are going to close. When it becomes too much of an effort to keep them open, let them close. If your mind remains alert and is analysing your progress, it will automatically bring the process of "letting go" to a stop. You must clear your mind—and keep it clear. Whatever noises occur do your best to disregard them—thoughts may drift into your mind, but gently push them out, and continue to let yourself rest and to become drowsier.

If the reader can obtain a crystal ball, set it on a stand, or hold it in the hands and regard it steadily with half-closed eyes. Similar results can be obtained by using a plain glass filled with water, or with a mirror. The same principles apply in each case. The lack of any specific point in distance on which to fix the eyes causes a slight disorientation, first of eye focus, and then of consciousness. This disorientation or detachment increases with suggestion. In the case of a crystal, the "depth of focus" will be the diameter of the crystal, as is also the case with a tumbler of water or, in the case of a mirror, the thickness of the glass. This can be seen if a mirror is closely examined. The mirror is silvered on the back of the glass. Thus, whilst gazing at the mirror, particularly if this is done from the angle of approximately 45 degrees, it will be found that the eyes are sometimes fixed on the surface of the mirror, that is, the front surface of the glass, or sometimes on the silver surface, which is the back of the glass, or sometimes wandering midway between these two planes. The effect produced by this method can produce a number of different reactions. Some people experience drowsiness, some may go off into a trance.

For this method, obtain a mirror and in the centre paste a small piece of white paper, about the size of a pea. If a hand mirror is being used, lay it flat on the table so that you can look into it easily, and without strain. If the mirror of a dressing table is being used, seat yourself comfortably and look steadily at the spot you have pasted on it. Push all other thoughts out of your mind, and remain gazing intently at the spot. Do not let your attention wander. The distance of the spot from your eyes should be one that is comfortable and causes no strain. It is better if the head and body lean forward slightly, so that the eyes have to look upwards a little. Soon your eyes will blink or grow heavy. If they remain fixedly open they will begin to smart and burn, and your vision will become blurred. Just continue gazing at the focal point and soon a strong desire to close your eyes will be felt. Do nothing—*don't think or try to analyse what is happening.* The point is reached when your eyes will close of their own accord—when this happens, let them remain closed and rest, and drowsiness will get deeper and deeper. Let it increase to the utmost point which is consistent with the retention of sufficient control to rouse yourself if you wish to break the trance. Having arrived at this state, continue to rest.

Another method is to lie down relaxed, having previously arranged for some small object such as a bright bead, a key or a button, to be suspended about a foot from one's face. This can be arranged by tying a piece of string or thread across the room from a window-catch to a picture-rail directly over where you are lying or sitting. A further string or thread should then be attached to hang vertically. At the end of this string, suspend the small object which should be in front of, or slightly above, your eye-level so that the eyes look upwards and converge slightly.

Regard the object steadily until the induced heaviness and drowsiness cause the eyes to close, then continue to let yourself become drowsier.

There are many other ways of employing this method of gaze fixation for trance induction. Almost any object will serve the purpose of acting as a fixed point on which you can focus both your eyes and your attention.

There are various mechanical aids to learning self-hypnosis, among which the fixed gaze contrivances such as revolving disks, lights, etc., can be helpful in the early stages of trance induction. The visual aids have the limitation of becoming inoperative after the eyes are closed, and it is here that the auditory aids such as listening to a metronome, or a clock ticking, have the advantage by maintaining a link with the student through his sense of hearing.

Undoubtedly the most helpful aid is a recorded hypnotic induction in which the student is conditioned and guided by the hypnotist through the lighter trance states into a deeper trance. As the student can listen to the recording whenever and as often as he wishes, the hypnotic conditioning is under his own control. A recorded course by the author is available which contains a hypnotic induction and post-hypnotic suggestions; the student will subsequently be able to induce the trance state in himself without the aid of the recording. Further details about these recordings and where they are available may be obtained by writing to the author.

From my own experience, the best and most convenient way of entering the trance state is an extension of the method described as the One, Two, Three Method described in Chapter Five. This can be carried out lying down or seated in a chair.

It will be found that if the previous instructions have been carried out by mentally counting One, Two, Three, the reflex will have been built where the eyes gently close by themselves at the count of Three, then with the eyes closed continue four, five, six, seven, eight, nine, ten. Whilst counting, a drift will have occurred towards the trance state. This can be deepened by one of the following disorientation exercises.

When you have arrived at "ten" whilst resting, and your eyes close, direct your attention to the top right-hand corner of the ceiling behind you. Pause for a few seconds, then direct your attention to the right-hand corner of the room in front of you, to the front left-hand corner, then behind left-hand corner and back to the starting point. As we are positioned in space and time through our senses when we close our eyes and begin these disorientation exercises, our mental appreciation begins to drift towards a trance or sleep state, and in this trance state you can make suggestions to yourself.

If the reader has attained only a light trance up to now, do not let him draw any negative conclusions about the ultimate outcome of his exercises. It cannot be repeated too often that suggestions can be effectively registered even in a very light trance.

The reader can now begin repeating suggestions to aid him in "letting go." Let him phrase general suggestions of ease—of being comfortable—of relaxing—of sinking down—of getting drowsier and drowsier—sleepier and sleepier, etc.

Another simple but effective method is to sit, or lie down and, when generally relaxed, begin slowly to count mentally to yourself. At the word "One" gently allow the eyes to close. At "Two" lazily open them. At "Three" close, and on "Four" open again. Continue counting and allowing the eyes to gently close on the odd numbers and opening them on the even numbers. When opening and closing the eyes do not do so jerkily but softly, letting them close, as it were, by themselves, and opening them smoothly and lazily. Before starting this method of induction, make the suggestion to yourself that your eyes are going to get heavier and heavier as you proceed, and before you have been counting very long they will be so heavy that it will be too much of an effort to open them. Continue counting until this occurs, and continue with suggestions as described in the previous method.

CHAPTER ELEVEN

TRANCE INDUCTION (Continued)

Feedback Method

This method is based on the fact that we ourselves are the best judge of the phrases or words which describe our inner sensations.

To operate this method, either write down or remember the phrases or words which were helpful in carrying out exercises – the phrases which seemed to "ring a bell." Maybe "Feel heavier ... warmer ... my breathing is getting deeper". . . and so on. This method,when relaxed, is to re-present to yourself as mental suggestions the feelings and sensations of relaxation and drowsiness which you have previously experienced. Frame these suggestions in such a manner as to intensify the effects; for example: "I am feeling heavier and heavier ... I am feeling warmer ... breathing getting deeper, the deeper my breathing and the heavier I feel, the drowsier I am becoming." To operate, seat yourself or lie down as previously described, and make the suggestions to yourself. When making the suggestions to yourself it is not necessary to speak them aloud; to repeat them mentally is sufficient. As this detachment grows, the reader will be growing nearer and nearer to the position where he is playing the dual role of hypnotist and subject.

Reading Method

This is a simple method of flooding the mind with one idea to the exclusion of everything else. It consists of writing down some descriptions of relaxation based on how you felt during your previous inductions. Choose all sensations and feelings which are conducive to furthering complete relaxation. As a suggested beginning, something on these lines might be employed: "I am sitting comfortably and am feeling at ease. I am resting and feeling very drowsy—If I go on reading this I shall get drowsier—My arms feel heavy and my body feels heavier—I am reading more slowly—My eyelids are getting heavier—I find it an effort to read. My eyes are getting heavier and I am beginning to feel sleepy—I am feeling very comfortable—My body is relaxed—My arms are relaxed—My legs feel heavy—My feet and legs feel relaxed, and heavy. All the while I am becoming more comfortable—and more deeply relaxed—I just want to rest—My eyes are getting heavier —So very heavy that I am closing them gradually. I want them to close—I just want to rest."

When you are going to employ this method for induction see that it is written clearly, or typed, so that it can be read easily and without effort. Seat yourself comfortably, preferably with a low light, and read it slowly. Read slowly as you become affected by the suggestions. When your eyes want to close, let them, and allow yourself to rest for a few seconds—continue to make mental suggestions of detachment and then register your current suggestions.

Saturation of the Attention Method

This method consists of completely saturating the mind with one idea. To make the procedure clear, it has already been explained that there are a number of different elements present in any state of mind, or that consciousness is an aggregate of many elements. This method consists of a number of separate processes which are practised, one by one, beforehand. The induction then becomes a

matter of performing all the separate processes simultaneously. If this is successfully carried out, the utmost
state of detachment consistent with retention of volition is
achieved.

To operate this method, take the idea of drowsiness as
the one with which we wish to flood the mind. Drowsiness
is chosen because it closely resembles the detached state of
mind which the reader wishes to produce in himself.

The first process is the physical disposition of the body,
as already dealt with in the first exercises on General
Relaxation. The second process is to call to mind the
general effects of drowsiness on the emotional state, its
pleasantness, disinclination to make effort, its detachment,
etc., which will already have been experienced in previous
exercises. For the third process, visualise in the mind's eye
the word "Drowsiness," as if it were printed in block letters on a piece of card, or, alternatively, if when experimenting you find it more efficacious, in your mind's eye
picture yourself sitting comfortably nearly asleep. For the
fourth process, practise saying the word "Drowsiness" or
"Drowsy" softly to yourself. In doing this, feel the movements of the lips and tongue as you say it. Say it softly,
slowly, lazily; say the words slowly. Mumble it if you wish.
For the fifth process, bring the sense of hearing consciously
into play. Listen to yourself saying the word Drowsy or
Drowsiness;.listen closely to each syllable.

The next step is to see that the word Drowsiness is
spoken as the act of breathing out is being made. See that
the breathing out of the word becomes a sleepy sigh. These
processes must, as far as possible, be practised separately
until they can be performed without effort or thought.

Preliminary practice will be necessary to produce and
marshal all these separate reflexes so that they may be
smoothly co-ordinated, without any reference to, or super-

vision from, the conscious mind. We cannot expect to get any trance conditions until the conscious mind is perfectly free from these supervisory tasks. Attempts to induce auto-hypnosis will fail until the conscious mind is free from the task of arranging these psycho-physical conditions, for the simple reason that it is an impossibility to keep the mind a blank and think of something at the same time.

When the reflexes have become automatic, the conscious mind then becomes a passive spectator of what is happening. This is the detachment that is felt and experienced when auto-hypnosis is about to be induced.

When carrying out this induction, sit or lie down, and relax, then begin gently and quietly saying the word Drowsy or Drowsiness . . . Feel the physical movements you are making with your tongue, lips, and those caused by your breathing . . . Hear yourself saying the words softly . . . In the mind's eye call up the picture you have chosen which is most strongly associated with drowsiness, i.e. the word printed on a card, or whatever mental picture you wish . . . Physically feel all the sensations of the suggested idea.

Continue this process, but each time the word is uttered, speak it more slowly, say it more softly, and let the intervals between saying it get longer and longer. It is, of course, not necessary to say it with every outgoing breath. If this process of co-ordination is carried out without any distractions, the whole mind, body and feelings will be subject to this one compulsive influence.

If the reader has conscientiously carried out the previous exercises he will have induced some degree of detachment, or trance condition. Even if only a light trance has been attained, give yourself suggestions that subsequent exercises will be successfully carried out, and the trance will become deeper.

Proceed without undue effort or haste. If results are slow in coming, face the fact. Follow the instructions carefully and conscientiously. Your progress may be rapid, or it may be slow. If the latter is the case, do not in any way be disturbed. If the exercises previously given are approached with the right attitude of mind, and are carefully carried out, it will not be long before sufficient detachment is achieved to successfully employ suggestion. By applying the re-presentation methods already described, a light trance can be steadily deepened.

Each of the methods described has terminated with the instruction to continue to become drowsier, or to rest. The depth of auto-hypnotic trance which is of the greatest value is that in which there is the maximum degree of detachment consistent, with retention of volition and "self control." It is a state in which the will is voluntarily suspended but sufficient volition is retained to terminate the trance if desired.

CHAPTER TWELVE

TRANCE DEEPENING

It is not at all necessary for the average reader wishing to cure some ailment, or to alter some condition or habit in his life, to master the trance deepening methods described in this section. I would emphasise that beneficial results are dependent on regular suggestions sessions, and frequent and realistic revisions of the suggestions. The methods in this section are primarily for students of psychological techniques, research, E.S.P. or meditational techniques, but many readers may wish to experiment with them.

The main causes which prevent trance induction, or the deepening of trances, are:—trying too hard and being over-anxious; employing induction methods which are not suitable to you; because your unconscious mind does not approve of the suggestions you wish to make; because unthinkingly you may have been making negative suggestions about your progress, or some form of unconscious resistance. The majority of these resistances can be overcome by following the advice given in this Course. In it, there is a great deal of information and instruction, but some readers may have to experiment with the various methods of trance induction described, perhaps making some alterations or modifications, or combining some of the different methods to find one which is suited to their individual circumstances and requirements.

When you experience only a slight feeling of detachment during practice, that is the time to make suggestions to yourself: your trance, however slight, will become deeper by using it, that is by repeating it and using positive suggestions. Do not say to yourself "This is not what I expected. This is not deep enough, I want a deep trance." Do not make it a condition that you must go into a deep trance before you begin suggestions. Remember that in any case the trance itself is only a means to an end; also remember that the majority of cures achieved by hypnotism are effected in medium and light trances. If you make it a definite condition that you must go into a deep trance it means you are, in effect, hypnotising yourself with the idea "I cannot get benefit until I go into a deep trance." This is untrue and there is no point in misleading yourself. The correct suggestion should be "Whether the trance I achieve is light, medium or deep I am going to get rid of (mention your difficulty) as soon as I possibly can." Do not lay down conditions. One of the main reasons for the resistance of the unconscious mind to trance induction is because the individual tries to force his unconscious mind. The way to deepen trances and one of the ways in which unconscious resistances are overcome is to make the right suggestions with gentle persistence ... do this, and the trance will become deeper by itself. If you try to force matters you will arrive at a deadlock.

A very light trance can be created by simply closing the eyes and mentally counting up to ten. Given the right conditions this trance will become progressively deeper, but, if immediately after the "ten" the individual says to himself "I am not in a trance, I am wide awake" he automatically brushes aside what would have developed into a trance. If instead of making the above mental comment to himself he had mentally noted a heaviness in his arms or legs (refer to the relaxation exercises given earlier) and had mentally said "I believe my arms are getting heavier and my breathing seems a little deeper," and if he had continued in this strain, the light trance would have become progressively deeper.

I met a man in India who performed some very impressive feats and I commented on the ease and speed with which he induced a trance in himself. I was surprised by his telling me that it was seven years from the time he first tried to induce a trance, before he succeeded. The reason for his taking this long time was because at his first attempts he had an expectation of being able to create a trance in a few sessions. When he failed to induce a trance fairly quickly, he was disappointed and lost heart and gave up his attempts for the time being. For some years he tried at intervals without success to induce a trance until he realised that his failure was because he had unthinkingly been making negative suggestions to himself and he had not been systematically practising but had simply been carrying out desultory experiments when he felt like it. Once he began to practise regularly, he soon succeeded.

Sometimes, as in the case of the man just mentioned, a student may come to a standstill and not know why. It may be that he has encountered some form of unconscious resistance or for some other reasons.

It is not possible, in a general course of this nature, to give precise instructions in every case, but if you are not making the progress your efforts merit and care to write, giving brief details to me at Home Farm Estate, Northchurch, Herts, I will be pleased to advise the best steps to take to overcome your difficulty.

With the majority of people deepening trance is a gradual process, but with patience and perseverance most resistances gradually resolve themselves. One cause of resistance to trance induction is that the unconscious mind takes exception to the nature of the suggestions made by the conscious mind. Often by altering the suggestions this unconscious resistance is overcome. For example, suppose a man is behind with his work and is overworking. If he begins to make suggestions to overcome feelings of fatigue and he is already drawing too deeply on his reserves of energy, his unconscious mind will veto his suggestions and he will have an unconscious resistance to trance and hypnotic suggestion. If this applies to any reader he will find the solution by re-reading the recommendations in the earlier part of the Course on how the co-operation of the unconscious can be obtained by framing the suggestions in such a way that they will be approved both by the conscious and the unconscious mind.

One method of trance deepening is to write down a description of the experiences of sinking into a trance. The reader can call on his imagination to aid him here, describing his feelings in drifting off into sleep and incorporating some of the suggestions given below. This is an elaboration of what has been described as "Feed back Method." The reason for the reader compiling the material himself is that it will be his own experiences in his own words. The following are suggestions of the lines on which these self suggestions are to be prepared: "I am sitting in a chair— My body feels heavy—I am feeling very tired—I don't want to make any effort—of any kind—I feel drowsy and relaxed—This drowsiness is becoming deeper—My eyes are closed—I feel a lethargy stealing over me—My thoughts are becoming slower and slower—It is just as though I were going to sleep—but I will be able to hear everything that goes on. My breathing is becoming slower, quieter and deeper. My whole system feels rested—My eyes feel very heavy—Emotionally I feel in a quiet, pleasant, contented state. I am physically and mentally completely relaxed—My legs are becoming heavier and heavier—My body, back and shoulders are relaxed—I have no desire to do anything—except rest—and let this drowsiness become deeper and deeper."

If the reader has difficulty in memorising, let him confine himself to short, simple repetitions. The reason for writing out the suggestions is to assist in remembering them. It is not necessary to be word perfect if the general theme expressed is one of deep relaxation. Let the reader select from the foregoing methods of induction the one from which he has experienced the best results. The next step is, when the maximum trance depth has been achieved, to employ the memorised material in the form of self-suggestions.

Take care that the clothing worn is loose-fitting and comfortable, and that you have bare feet, or comfortable shoes or slippers. It may be found helpful to have a light covering, a travelling rug or quilt, spread over you to ensure there are no draughts so that you are not cold. Pay particular attention to the temperature of the room and, if necessary, see that it is reasonably warm beforehand, and that it is not draughty. Arrange as far as you can that before the sessions there has been no abnormal expenditure of energy, that you have not been drawing deeply on your reserves of nervous energy. The purpose of this instruction is, if possible, to ensure that your level of nervous energy is not depleted or below normal, as this tends to increase tension. Some people find that to take off their shoes and place a hot water bottle at their feet is conducive to a trance, but by making these physical arrangements for comfort, the risk of going to sleep is increased.

A warm bath is very helpful, but with some people it will create the wrong conditions for trance induction. It is not possible to give specific instructions which will serve as a guide to everyone. Each individual reacts in a different way, in consequence of which the reader is advised to make a close and detailed study of his own reactions. By self-observation he may possibly detect many small circumstances which will, without his knowledge, have been mildly disturbing him. For example, one student who practised his exercises in the late evening had failed to make any headway beyond light trance, and discovered that when he left off drinking tea in the evening the tension which he had previously experienced vanished immediately. The reader is recommended to study very closely all circumstances and actions which are likely to influence his attempts.

If the trance state goes too deep, the reader will only become aware of this when he wakes up. There is no record or evidence of anyone ever experiencing any inconvenience through self-induced trance. If, whilst carrying out the exercise, the reader enters a deep trance or falls fast asleep, he must, at the next session, induce a medium trance in which he does not allow himself to sink too deeply, and direct suggestions to prevent himself from losing control. These suggestions should be on the following lines: "I am sinking down into a trance, but I will not go to sleep, nor will I lose consciousness. I will be aware of any noises which go on outside, but they will not disturb me, and I will hear them all the while. The object of my practice and exercises is to implant suggestions in my unconscious mind and so that I shall be able to do this I must not lose consciousness or go to sleep."

It cannot be repeated too often that to effect alterations in oneself it is not necessary to hypnotise oneself. This course teaches how all the alterations which can be brought about in a self-induced trance can be achieved through self-suggestion.

The following exercise in disorientation is helpful in increasing depth of trance. It can be practised as a preliminary to a suggestion session.

Darkened Room. This preliminary exercise is to be carried out in total darkness. Complete darkness is employed in the training of insangomas (and many other mystics). In these cases the nature of the trance is different for it becomes possible to open the eyes without disturbing the trance (this is somnambulism). To reach this state a great deal of time and practice is necessary. It is difficult to maintain the delicate balance between either going off in unconsciousness and sleep or alternatively to become roused and alert. Practice this exercise in a completely darkened room. Experiment by walking about with a short stick in your hand and finding your way by touching objects with the end of the stick and very rapidly you will experience the sensation that you are "feeling" with the end of the stick. This is the beginning of a sensory extension. After you have carried out this experiment with both hands lie down with your eyes closed and place a forefinger *gently* on your eyelid and very, very gently apply pressure. If you move your finger when you touch certain spots you will probably see some flashes of light, possibly coloured lights. This is caused by pressure on the optic nerve and is to be carried out very gently indeed. Now remove your hands and mentally concentrate in the mind's eye, trying to re-visualise the flashes of light, without of course in any way touching your eyes. Keep your eyes closed while you are doing this. These vague shadowy half lights which are seen sometimes when the eyes are closed are the raw material out of which mental images are formed. They can also be formed by concentration. Turn your attention to try to build up images of the numeral one, see it like the Number 1 on a blackboard, that is, as a white figure against a black background. When you have seen this, even if it is only vague, cancel it out and make the Number 2 appear. Cancel this and continue creating each number up to 10. The purpose of this exercise is not only of mental control but it also produces a dis-orientation and it will be found, as a result of this and the following trance deepening exercise, that the depth of your trances will be improved.

For this trance deepening exercise, lie down with your arms at your side and close your eyes. Do not try to create a trance but simply imagine a point moving round the outlines of your body. Begin at the crown of your head and imagine the point moving down the side of your head, tracing the outline of your ear, then down the side of your neck, along your shoulder, down the outside of your arm, until you come to the top of your little finger. Then trace the line in between your fingers, around your thumb, up the inside of your arm, to your armpit, and then continue tracing the outline of your body until you have returned to the crown of your head. And continue with trance deepening suggestions.

CHAPTER THIRTEEN

OVERCOMING OBSTACLES

An obstacle in learning to hypnotise oneself can arise if the student has an exaggerated idea of what he imagines he will experience during the trance state. Not many people have the expectation of entering some strange mystical mental state and being wafted off to some indefinable realms, but sometimes preconceived ideas of what the trance state is, can hinder rather than help progress. If a student is trying to attain something which has no existence except in his own imagination this will obviously hinder his progress in the attainment of a real trance state.

Another obstacle can arise because students of self-hypnosis very frequently underestimate the degree in which they have been affected in their practise sessions. It is an established fact that people tend to underestimate the depth of trance they have attained. Readers who are acquainted with text books on hypnosis will be well aware that frequently the subject's assessment of how far he had been hypnotised is quite incorrect. This is often due to an expectation of some strange experience and even when therapeutic benefits or post-hypnotic suggestions are a demonstrable proof that hypnosis has been achieved, the subject will sometimes stubbornly maintain that he has not been hypnotised.

These two obstacles of undervaluation of progress and expectation of some mysterious experience during the trance state can be avoided by keeping an open mind in assessing and evaluating progress made in any particular session. This is achieved by avoiding negative comments such as "I am not doing this well," or "I'm not making progress."

The fact is that the trance state can vary vastly according to the mental and emotional attitude of the individual at the time he is carrying out a trance induction session. During the session he may be discharging muscular or emotional tensions and so appear to be restless and it may seem to him that he is not making progress, whereas in actual fact he is making real and positive steps towards achieving relaxation, emotional equilibrium and the trance state. On the other hand, he may just relax and sink peacefully into a pleasant lethargic state. To avoid being influenced by the "ups and downs" which may be encountered in suggestion sessions, it is wise to avoid any negative comments and concentrate on carrying out regular suggestion sessions.

In all cases the trance state is characterised by a sense of remoteness, but this does not mean losing consciousness.

Volitional control is never lost in the self-hypnotic trance state. If self-control is lost it is no longer self-hypnosis, for the individual drifts into a deeper trance which immediately turns into ordinary sleep from which he will wake in a normal manner. The length of time he sleeps will depend on how tired and comfortable he is and what external distractions are going on and what waking suggestions he has made to himself before beginning the suggestions session.

It is difficult to define mental and emotional states and conditions, but we can get some idea of what the trance state is if we examine a little more closely what happens when we go to sleep.

Actually it is not as though we were wide awake one moment and unconscious the next . . . though sometimes we appear to drop off to sleep suddenly. In reality, just before we lose consciousness, we pass rapidly through what in psychological language is called a hypnogogic condition; also in waking we pass through a somewhat similar condition described as hypnopompic. Both these states are hypnoidal trance states but they are both of such brief duration that normally during them, or subsequently on waking, we have no memory of them.

The self-hypnotic trance state is induced by letting yourself sink beneath the surface of the mind or to withdraw awareness from the outside world into oneself until the focal point of awareness approaches the boundary which divides the conscious from the unconscious mind and to remain poised or suspended in this detached trance state.

The whole art is to remain mentally poised, not rising to the surface, for if we do we break the sense of detachment, nor sinking too deep for then we drift into oblivion. In this state, with practise, we learn to retain sufficient awareness to remain linked with the outside world. In this state or condition our Intellect and our Will lie ready at hand to be used if we wish to make the effort. If we remain quiescent in this suspended trance state we have achieved what Krishnamurti has called "Choiceless Awareness," and if we use self-hypnosis positively we allow suggestions, or possibly supplications, to pass through our minds. I say *allow*, for our suggestions are the voicing of our needs, our hopes, our wishes and desires arising from the depths of our being.

It sounds paradoxical to say that many people wishing to learn self-hypnosis have already been, to all intents and purposes, hypnotised without their knowing it; that is to say that their real objective in learning self-hypnosis is to *dehypnotise* themselves from some negative ideas or emotions.

Negative suggestions which have been put into a man's or woman's mind by someone else can ruin their lives, and frequently people are unaware that their shortcomings are due to the operation of damaging post-hypnotic suggestions acquired as a result of a shock or accident. It has to be kept in mind that negative ideas and suggestions can be registered in the unconscious mind without the induction of a trance, and also that the victim may or may not consciously remember them.

A typical experience of this was related to me by a woman who, after her stepmother's death, had resigned herself to a lonely life in which work and worry were predominant. In her childhood her stepmother had unceasingly criticised her, telling her that she was stupid and ugly and that no man would ever look at her. When the stepmother died she was left alone, fearful and filled with feelings of inferiority. She had, to all intents and purposes, been brainwashed.

In her own quiet way she tried to help herself for she felt as though some invisible barrier was holding her back and preventing her from living an ordinary life. One night she went to a lecture on psychology where the lecturer carried out some experiments in hypnosis. Being a suggestible subject she responded well to his suggestions and was hypnotised. The hypnotist told her she would feel very confident and, for the first time in her life the woman experienced what it was like to feel free from fear and feelings of inferiority.

She went away from the lecture feeling that a new life was opening up for her. Unfortunately her new found confidence lasted only for a few days, but she knew from this experience that, even if it were only for a short time, it was possible to shed her fears, and she resolved to learn all she could about hypnosis. She attempted to get in touch with the lecturer but her letters were unanswered, so she began to read all she could about the subject.

She wrote to me telling me what had occurred at the lecture and asking me if I would teach her to hypnotise herself. I taught her how to create the trance state in herself and instructed her how she could remove the effects of past negative conditioning and build herself a new life.

This woman's experience was typical of the process of dehypnotisation ... in fact it could be said she had experienced four different types of hypnotic conditioning.

The first was the negative conditioning of her stepmother constantly telling her that she was slow, stupid and awkward. Despite the fact that no formal trance had been induced, the negative suggestions had been so effectively registered in the child's unconscious mind that, like a hypnotised subject, she had been acting out the stepmother's post-hypnotic suggestions all her life. She had felt, acted and experienced exactly as her stepmother had said she would, and in fact had become the person her stepmother had said she would become.

The second phase was when the lecturer's hypnotic suggestions of confidence had temporarily cancelled out the stepmother's negative influence.

The third phase was when I hypnotised her in the course of teaching her how to hypnotise herself.

The fourth phase was when she began to use self-hypnosis to remove all traces of the negative conditioning she had received in childhood, and for the first time to really express her own personality.

The purpose of relating this case history is to draw

attention to the fact that probably most hypnotic suggestions are concerned with removing damaging or negative ideas, emotions, attitudes or habits and DEHYPNOTISING people from influences which prevent them from leading fuller lives.

As many readers will already know, or will have gathered from my former comments about using recordings to learn self-hypnosis, if a subject is hypnotised by a hypnotist (or a hypnotic recording) and hypnotic suggestions are made to him that later he (the subject) will be able to hypnotise himself, then he will be able to do so. This sounds like a wonderful short cut, but there is rather more in learning self-hypnosis than being hypnotised and having post-hypnotic suggestions made to one by a hypnotist.

It is true that one can learn self-hypnosis in this way but it is inadvisable to do so without first acquiring some knowledge of the subject. Self-hypnosis is a potent power which, like most powers, can be misused. In the hands of someone who has no self-knowledge, self-hypnosis is like a learner driver in charge of a powerful racing car. I saw an example of this misuse when a man who was an excellent hypnotic subject had a very badly poisoned foot. He was a mechanic who had spilt some melted solder on his foot and had given himself hypnotic suggestions that his foot would not pain him and that he would forget all about it. He successfully blocked out the pain and by ignoring nature's warning had a badly poisoned foot. I am not suggesting that the average individual would be as imprudent as this, but those learning self-hypnosis should learn how they can use and direct the power they are acquiring.

In learning self-hypnosis there is a development of co-ordination between mental and emotional processes which is akin to the development of the body through physical exercise; the acquisition of psychological instead of physical skills. The ability to withdraw into oneself in even a light trance is not a kind of psychological trick but a skill which, like other skills, improves with practise.

There is no reason why a hypnotist's aid should not be called upon to help in learning self-hypnosis, but it should be remembered that if the ability is acquired through the post-hypnotic suggestions of someone else, the initiation (if I can call it that) should be followed by regular daily sessions to bed down the habit and make it one's own before the post-hypnotic suggestions fade, which they will tend to do unless practice in trance induction is carried out for some weeks.

The soundest course to follow would be to practise on the lines set out in the foregoing pages and if, for some reason or other, progress seems slow and the help of a hypnotist is available, there is no reason why his help should not be called upon.

I have, as far as possible, avoided making personal references to myself, but I feel it would be helpful to mention that in acquiring my own knowledge of the subject I spent some nine years overseas in Africa and India, visiting many mystics, witch doctors, sadhus and indigenous healers who were practising what I am convinced were various forms of hypnosis. In India the techniques are known as *moorchana shastrum* or *vashee karana vidya*. In the Arab world it is known as *Tanweem*. In most places I visited I found versions of hypnosis or self-hypnosis.

This strange psychological phenomena is not explained by giving it a name as did Dr. Braid when he christened it hypnosis any more than electricity or atomic energy is explained by naming them; we can see their manifestations but the hidden mystery eludes us.

I found during my travels that most healing methods demanded on the part of those who sought help, belief in a Saint, a God, a holy relic, an image or a shrine, and in many cases a trance state was experienced by devotees. All faiths bring about improvements in some of their followers . . . but it does appear that as man's critical faculty develops, his ability to give himself up unreservedly in this simple act of faith diminishes. It seems that as man's reason develops, it weakens his faith and, for a time, puts nothing in its place. This I believe is an inevitable stage in development, and I also believe we are now living in an age which is seeing the dawn of new Mental Sciences. Foremost amongst these, and within the grasp of anyone who wishes to explore these new fields, is self-hypnosis. It is an uncommitted faith. . . it asks nothing except the courage to explore new methods and keep an open mind.

CONCLUSION

IN THIS LAST SECTION THERE ARE A NUMBER OF POINTS
WHICH MAY BE FOUND HELPFUL AS ADVICE OR REMINDERS.

Do not be uneasy or doubtful about "coming to" or
"waking up" from any of the states of consciousness which
are induced. Before you begin exercises, estimate what
time you have available—just think to yourself: "I've
got half-an-hour to spend," (or whatever the period may
be). Impress the thought on your mind, and carry on with
your exercise. Although you have apparently pushed away
the thought, there is a part of your mind which will
prompt you when the period is nearing its end. If the
conscious mind had forgotten the time, your sub-conscious
mind would remind you.

— — — — —

When practising your self-suggestion sessions do not be
uneasy about going into a very deep trance. If this did
happen, the experience is somewhat similar to that of
dropping off to sleep. The deep trance state will turn into
a normal sleep from which, after a brief rest, you will
wake in a perfectly normal manner.

— — — — —

The most convenient times to employ self-suggestion are
immediately after waking, and just before going to sleep.
Generally speaking, auto-suggestions are not so effective
when energy level is low, though our impressionability to
suggestions from others is increased. It is good practice
to follow a regular routine, spending three or four minutes
every morning and night on constructive suggestions.

If during your first few sessions you become aware of various tensions . . . do not feel in any way disturbed. This is a part of the process of unwinding. Repressed tensions have to go somewhere, some subside and others discharge themselves when the will is switched off and you "let go." If a muscle twitches or you feel a vague restlessness, as far as you can disregard these tensions rising to the surface, think to yourself "I'm pleased to get rid of that," and carry on with your exercise. The tensions may continue to arise for a few sessions but will soon disappear.

— — — — —

It is essential to direct suggestions towards the removal of negative attitudes which have arisen as a result of reverses or disappointments. From day to day incorporate in your suggestions, varying ideas to the effect that your exercises will yield progressive benefits.

— — — — —

Never forget that pain and fatigue are nature's signals for attracting our attention. Suggestions should not be used to cancel out these signals before ascertaining their causes. Do not remove symptoms of pain or fatigue unless you are sure it is wise to do so. ALWAYS OBTAIN A MEDICAL OPINION REGARDING ANY SUSPICIOUS OR PERSISTENT PAIN OR SYMPTOM.

— — — — —

Repeat suggestions whilst fully awake. Repeat them as rapidly as possible. Tie twenty knots in a piece of string and carry this about with you in your pocket or handbag. This is a useful reminder to practice your suggestions, and by passing a knot between your finger and thumb each time a suggestion is made, it can be used to check the number of times the suggestions are repeated.

During self-observation, you will have noticed that there are some sayings which seem to give strength and support. Make a note of any which appeal to you. It does not matter how simple, platitudinous or colloquial they may be, such as: "It's a good thing I've got a sense of humour," or: "There are plenty of people worse off than I am," or: "I've been through worse troubles than this," or: "This can't go on forever." Simple statements of this nature have given people powerful aid when they desperately needed it. Though these suggestions are palliative in nature they have valuͤ as perspective correctors, and in sustaining morale.

The length of the suggestion sessions can be of comparatively short duration when progress has been made with the exercises. This is due to the fact that the time taken for getting into a suggestible state of mind is shortened, and experimentation is no longer necessary. Some people, once the habit of "letting go," or "putting oneself off," has been acquired, are able to put themselves into a medium depth of trance in a few seconds. When this stage has been arrived at, one or two minutes are ample for suggestion sessions. Until then, the major part of the time is spent in learning how to induce this stage of heightened suggestibility. This will account for approximately nine-tenths of the time which, in the early stages, is taken up in studying the technique. At the beginning, practically the whole of the time is taken up by relaxation exercises, and very little self-treatment is given, but once a trance or the detached state can be created, practically all the time is occupied in registering impressions.

As an exercise in auto-hypnosis and self-suggestion, take advantage of the well-known fact that, by impressing on your mind the idea that you will wake at a certain hour the next morning, you are likely to do so. This is best carried out immediately before sleeping. The ability to successfully effect these projected orders grows with practice.

When making suggestions to yourself take your time, express them aloud or mentally. The thoughts must flood the whole mind to the exclusion of everything else. There must be no thinking, no analysing, no self-observation about whatever you are saying: no self-criticism. All the thinking and all the analysing should have been done beforehand. Make and accept the suggestions you are putting to yourself, with conviction. Give yourself up to the belief that what you are saying is so, in every respect. The more you are able to surrender yourself to these suggestions, the stronger your conviction will grow.

Self-Hypnotism, or Auto-suggestion, is a means to an end. The life of any individual should be lived, arranged and organised, in full waking consciousness. Self-hypnotism and suggestion are only a means of building the habits necessary to live in a healthy, balanced manner.

If, when carrying out an exercise, for some reason you wish to suspend operations, do not hesitate or be irresolute. Decisively stop your exercise and postpone it as a definite act of will. This definite action on your part will prevent your being affected by negative suggestions, as you might be if the exercises continued in a desultory fashion, and deteriorated into a half-hearted attempt.

Having read through the whole of the work the reader is now advised, if he has not already done so, to commence practical work on the exercises. He is also advised, in addition to carrying out the exercises, to re-read the

Course at intervals, as each time it is read further information may be gained which was not apparent at earlier readings.

As the days pass, devote what time you can to a routine of regular Suggestion Sessions .... observing yourself ... reflecting on any amendments or additions to the suggestions you are making ... and incorporating these in your next suggestion session. Changes will be observed. A life undergoing a transformation is often like a garden growing. The changes are sometimes slow and imperceptible ... sometimes dramatic and startling, but whether they are slow or rapid, improvements depend on individual cases. Stomach ulcers can be cured but the tissue changes take time. Hidden obstacles will come to light, self-created difficulties may become apparent, but so also will the methods for dealing with these difficulties, methods of which the individual would never have consciously thought. It will soon be discovered that the unconscious mind has far greater wisdom than the conscious mind. If with sincerity we call on the unconscious mind, or the Unknown, it will soon be discovered that we are indeed invoking powers truly capable of performing miracles. The method of bringing into operation these powers is extremely simple—we must sincerely direct efforts to freeing within ourselves the mighty powers which are the source of all life. If what we are trying to achieve is for our good and in accord with the creative forces which work through all life, it will not be long before, through our co-operation with these forces, we are enjoying a harmonious way of life.

It should be borne in mind that unexpected circumstances may arise which will interfere with, or upset the arrangements you have planned for practice sessions. Should temporary setbacks of this nature be encountered, it must be remembered that you are no longer dealing with your difficulties with the simple outlook of one who believes that he must either be a success or a failure, but with the enlightened outlook of one who knows his limitations and is overcoming them by consciously choosing the suggestions which determine his attitude of mind and actions, and who is not letting chance and circumstances choose them for him. With this thought in mind, do temporary setbacks really matter . . . so long as the goal is eventually reached?

In the beginning of this Course I said that anyone thrown on his own resources to overcome some problem or ailment, would, once he finds the way, emerge from the ordeal far stronger than he was before.

Faith and belief sustain us in our hour of need, but because of the complexity of some of the problems with which we are faced today, our faith needs reinforcing with understanding. Man is conquering the forces of nature in the outside world through his knowledge of the laws of nature, and in the same way many people are curing psychosomatic ills, resolving conflicts and developing their latent abilities through a knowledge of the laws which govern their own mental and emotional life.

We do not need to understand the nature of thought or emotion, any more than we need to know the nature of electricity in order to direct and harness its power. In this Course is set out a system of redirecting and harnessing our mental and emotional energies, so that they may flow into their predestined channels and, in this way, we may achieve physical well-being and peace of mind.